AF405586

DEEP WATER

BRITT HALAAS

Copyright © 2023 by Britt Halaas

All rights reserved.

No part of this publication may be reproduced, distributed, or transmitted in any form or by any means, including photocopying, recording, or other electronic or mechanical methods, without the prior written permission of the publisher, except as permitted by U.S. copyright law. For permission requests, contact Britt Halaas at britt.halaas@gmail.com.

The story, all names, characters, and incidents portrayed in this production are fictitious. No identification with actual persons (living or deceased), places, buildings, and products is intended or should be inferred.

Book Cover by @art_iseyaaaa

Edited by Kyare Betzing

First edition 2023

To Christina and Adam, the two friends I met on a cruise when I was 13 that provided some of the fun stories in this book. I never forgot about you!

CONTENT WARNINGS:

- Being outed without consent
- Toxic relationship with a parent
- Mentions of body size
- Non-main character divorce
- Non-main character pregnancy

CHAPTER 1

LORI

"I'm going into a hostage situation," I muttered as I stared at the huge cruise ship. What would normally be someone's dream vacation, was going to be hell for me. A hand touched my shoulder as the humidity in the air, and this whole situation made it harder and harder to breathe.

"Don't freak out." Ryan's deep voice came from behind me. Ryan had been my best friend for the last five years. He was the epitome of tall, dark, and handsome. He was going to make some man very happy one day. He let go of my shoulder to wipe sweat from his forehead.

"It's hard not to freak out. I'm bringing my best friend who's pretending to be my fiancé onto a cruise ship for a week to prove to my family that I won't die alone." *Yup, that's me. I am one of those serial single ladies that doesn't care if a man puts a ring on it. At least for the last few years.*

That didn't mean that I wasn't lonely sometimes.

"Lori." He gave me that face again. It was half irritation and half pity. It wasn't an unusual expression from him. He would often look at me like that whenever I thought poorly of myself. Sometimes, I think he loved me more than any straight man could.

"The shocking truth, I probably will!" I didn't want to be here; I didn't want to go on that ship and be trapped with the woman that had always downplayed who I wanted to be because it didn't fit into her plan for me. "I am already feeling claustrophobic." I sighed as I turned and looked up at the massive cruise ship. I felt hopeless.

"It's a huge ship and we will be on a vast ocean." Ryan joined me, looking up. I was barely even able to see the deck. He glanced back at me with confusion. "Are you afraid your mom is going to shove you in a closet or something?"

I glared as I deliberately turned to him, "I am about to be trapped on that ship on the vast ocean with my *family*."

"Cleithrophobia." He didn't look at me when he said it, he just kept looking at the ship.

"What?"

He smirked in my direction, "The fear of being trapped is cleithrophobia, not claustrophobia."

He was lucky I needed him because, at that moment, I was about to push him off the ramp that we were gradually making our way up as people ahead of us checked into the ship.

But this was the way our relationship had always been. We had developed a sibling-like relationship and bickered as such. However, on the other end of the spectrum, we would die for each other. He was the perfect best friend. We were each other's soulmates.

As we finally made our way to the front of the line, I was able to get my first good look at the dark industrial entrance of the ship, suddenly opening before us like the maw of some eldritch beast, the suction of which seemed to be stripping my soul. My parents paid for the whole trip because my mother loved showing off their wealth even to their children, "Let's just get this over with."

Two men stood at the opening of the ship. They were dressed in uniform and seemed friendly, but still rather intimidating.

I handed one of them my boarding pass and passport. My body tensed, and tingles ran up my back, realizing I was about to step into my personal hell. I dreaded spending time with my mother because she had been a very toxic person throughout my entire life. I hated the fact that I was going to be forced to see her for the next seven days and knew I would escape from her as much as possible.

"Welcome aboard, miss." The man shuffling through my paperwork had an Australian accent, my favorite. I can pick it out from just a word. Suddenly, I wasn't so nervous. I took in just how attractive he was. His dark hair, perfect profile, that accent. *Yeah, the Australian accent does that to me.*

"Thank you." I flirtatiously smiled at him.

Ryan placed his hands on my shoulders and pushed me forward. He flashed his boarding pass and passport to the sexy Australian man as he pushed me onto the ship. "If I can't hit on hot foreign men, then neither can you."

I couldn't help but laugh as Ryan pushed me through the entrance of the ship and down the hallway leading toward the passenger section.

We made our way into the grand room. It was huge. There were boutiques, eateries, and basically, everything you would need to live on this ship. It was beautiful. To my left, a grand staircase made of white marble rose three levels in an atrium style.

"Am I dead? Did we die?" Ryan's eyes were wide, and his jaw was practically on the ground. He walked slightly ahead of me and peered up to the skylight.

"No, somehow, this is reality." I patted him on his shoulder. "Come on. We gotta find the room, unpack, and meet my family on the Riviera deck to wave at people."

Ryan stopped and cocked his head. "Wave at people? Who?"

I grabbed his wrist and pulled him toward the staterooms. "People wishing us well on our trip." It seemed so normal to me, growing up with money was an interesting experience. I often forget that others didn't live like I lived. Vacations every year that involved a plane, sometimes a ship like this, other times a person in a mouse costume. Once I went to college, I learned that the way I lived was different.

"Who do you know in Fort Lauderdale?" he asked as he pulled away from my grasp to walk on his own.

I stopped and stared blankly into Ryan's eyes. "Absolutely no one." I knew how crazy it had sounded. I had been on a couple of cruises before; Ryan had not. "Listen, it's a cruise ship thing. You wave at the people who are on the shore, and they wave back."

Ryan was speechless. He was born and raised in New York City and had lived in LA for six years. He wasn't used to people randomly waving at others for no reason.

I grabbed his hand again and pulled him in the direction of our stateroom. "At least my parents got us a balcony room. I did offer to pay for it," I complained as we entered our room. It was small but comfortable. There was one king-size bed in the middle and a TV mounted on the wall opposite the bed. Aside from that, it was sparse. I had become very successful with an animation company. I was head art director for a hit cartoon on television and Ryan was one of my animators. I knew hanging out with your employees was the worst idea ever, but he and I became friends before I got this job when we were both background animators for a cartoon that lasted two years and then just went away. He and I could have afforded our own tickets, but my mother insisted on paying for both of us.

"I'm surprised your parents requested a single," Ryan mentioned as he tossed his suitcase on the large bed.

"I guess you're only expected to stay a virgin before marriage until your late 20s." I joked about my mother's random change in tone once I reached the age where I was now "running out of time" and that I might become an "old spinster." Somehow, my mother still lived in the days when a woman's only purpose was to pop out children. Truth was, and my mother would probably burst into flames if she knew, the virginity ship sailed at sixteen when I made a mistake with my first boyfriend. "I just wish she would have let me pay."

My parents have always been the kind of people who loved flaunting their money. My dad is a real estate agent, and my mother is a financial advisor. I grew up in Burnsville, Minnesota. Oh, you haven't heard of it? It's about seventeen miles directly south of Minneapolis, get on Interstate 35W heading North—sorry the Twin Cities are weird with their roads—and you just keep going until you hit downtown, that is if the construction isn't too bad.

With those jobs in the biggest population area of the entire state, they had money and a lot of it. They were also great at saving, so when the recession hit in 2008, it could have been devastating, but the truth is, we were fine, lived off my parents' savings for a few years until business picked back up again, and my dad became an expert in foreclosed houses during that time. The only downside was, I turned sixteen that year and I didn't get my dream car. It was devastating back then, but looking back, I was a spoiled brat.

So, it was clear that my parents were making sure us kids never forgot that they had money. Since they became empty nesters, they decided to spend our inheritance before we could ever get our greedy hands on it. This time, we were celebrating my dad for selling some famous athlete's multi-million-dollar property. It was the biggest house of his career, with the biggest commission.

"Oh, poor you, your parents are rich, and you just *have* to go on these vacations that you don't have to pay for." Ryan would often call me on my shit, I was still somewhat disconnected from reality when it came to money and no money. "I mean, come on, I had to get a job at fifteen to help pay for rent because of the recession."

I gazed over at Ryan; I had no idea that his family had that little money growing up. "You had to help pay rent?" I couldn't even imagine. I didn't have to start working until I got to college, but even then, it was mostly just spending money and not out of necessity. I spent my after-school time doing theater and mock trials. I wanted to be a lawyer when I was in high school. We spent summers camping, swimming, taking long bike trips, and all kinds of other outdoor activities where a summer job would have been impossible.

"Yeah, rent is this thing where you don't own a house —"

I cut him off. "I know what rent is!" My hands hugged my hips and my gaze pierced through him. I softened though. "It's just sad. You didn't get to enjoy stuff."

"Don't feel bad for me." I could tell I was making him angry. "I still had fun. I spent all my free time drawing," he explained.

It was then that I realized, I never listened to him. I had heard all his big accomplishments, graduating high school at the top of his class, getting accepted into the best animation school in the country, and coming out to his parents when he was twenty. "Why don't you ever talk about when you're a kid?" It's as if his life began at eighteen when he graduated high school.

Ryan shrugged but remained silent.

The ringing of my stateroom phone finally broke this awkward silence. I grabbed the phone quickly. "Hello?"

On the other end was my mother. "Hello, dear, glad to know you're on the ship, come to the deck so we can wave at the people on shore." It was my mother's favorite part of cruises. We had been on our fair share. Caribbean, Alaskan, Mediterranean, Nordic, you name it, we had done it at least once. We even once took a cruise on the Great Lakes—yes those exist.

"Yeah, I'll head right up there." I was always so used to being a singular person, I forgot I had Ryan with me.

"What about Ryan?" She sounded as though she had just heard the scandal of the century.

"He seemed to think the idea was pretty silly, but I'll see if he's ready to meet everyone." I glanced at Ryan who was unpacking his suitcase into one of the drawers.

"See you soon!" She sounded so proud of me like I had won an Oscar for best animated film or something. However, my winning an Oscar wouldn't mean anything to her if I didn't have a man to thank in my acceptance speech.

My mother meant well, or at least that's what I told myself. Her goal in life was to always have a successful marriage and happy healthy children. She only started working when all of us were in school. She was so desperate to be so intertwined with our growth and education, that she *needed* to be a stay-at-home mom. Maybe that's where I get my resentment for the idea of ever having children. Since I was a kid, I was always immersed in extracurricular activities. I had one boyfriend in high school that lasted two months and caused me to have sex before I was ready. My sister ended up marrying her high school sweetheart before either of them could drink at the reception. Don't get me wrong, I'm proud of them for the life they built, but that is not a life I would have wanted to live. I barely want to live it now. Then there was my brother. He dated casually until he met his current wife.

"Lori, honey, the only way to live a fulfilled life is to have children." That's what my mother would always tell me. From the moment I was eighteen, she was obsessed with getting me married because I was so far behind Kasey, my sister, that it was embarrassing for her, or something.

I mean, for her, that was true. I never wanted to devalue what she did and how she chose to live her life. It was just as valid of a choice as any. The issue always was, she never understood or validated how I wanted to live mine. Every time I would come home to visit, she would ask me about my love life, and now that I'm entering my thirties, I am evidently "running out of time."

"Lori." I had gotten lost in my head again. I did that a lot when I was preparing to see my family. There's a lot of resentment inside of me, hence my decision a few years ago to finally start seeing a therapist who had diagnosed me with a grocery list of conditions stemming from purity culture and my mother's emotional abuse.

"What?" I shook my head and looked at Ryan. He had managed to change into shorts and a tank top while I spoke with my mother and fell down this rabbit hole of dealing with how much my mother drove me crazy.

"I take it your mom wants to wave at strangers now?" He chuckled.

I knew he thought it seemed silly, but it was something fun to do. I hoped he would come with me and experience the fun himself. "Yeah, she wants you to come."

Ryan reached out his arm for me to wrap mine around. "Let's get this over with, fiancée."

I felt sick to my stomach at his words. "People don't talk like that, Ry." I didn't want him to blow our cover on the first night.

We made our way through the ship and got to the deck to meet my parents, and there was my eccentric mother with two margaritas in hand. Her burnt-umber hair was pulled back in a low ponytail. Her sunglasses are so big, you'd think she was a celebrity hiding her identity.

"One of those better be for me," I joked as I held out my hand with a sarcastic smile. She drove me crazy, but I also cultivated a play-nice attitude around her. I learned how to just nod and take her constant passive-aggressiveness about my life choices and not start a fight.

She handed me one of the drinks and I immediately began sucking that straw like I hadn't seen water in days. I was feeling like this was a multiple-drink night... I mean day. As I said, I learned how not to start a fight, and sometimes, that meant getting drunk by noon.

"Woah, slow down there, it's still technically morning." My baby brother laughed as he pulled the large green drink away from me. In his other hand, a bottle of beer.

Derrek, my brother, was three years younger than me, he had a wife, but no kids. I often wonder if Mom gave him the same crap, or if that's just saved for me.

"I do what I want." I messed with his sandy-colored hair. "Drink your beer and mind your own business." I stole my drink back and inhaled it once again. The plan was just to be drunk the whole week. That would probably make the trip a lot more tolerable.

We had a very playful relationship. He was one of my best friends growing up. I was surprised when he brought home a girl. He had always confided in me that he wasn't sure if he liked girls, boys, or both. I was very happy that he had found someone to love though. It was important to him. He was kind of like my mom that way. He knew from a young age that he wanted to get married and have children.

"What are you drinking, Steph?" I peered over to my sister-in-law, who had a clear drink. She had always been a party girl since I had known her. She and my brother started dating in college and got married very quickly. They would come out to California, and we would party hop. She had pictures with so many minor celebrities, you'd think she was one herself.

"Just water." Steph removed her sun hat, revealing her curly red hair. She's one of those cheerleader types from high school, but the ones that were nice to everyone, and not in an ironic way. I genuinely loved her.

"Water? Wanna go hard tonight?" I asked. I figured I had a built-in party group this week, and I was so looking forward to letting loose.

Steph and Derrek exchanged glances. "I can't."

Can't? What did that mean? "You can't?" I laughed. "What are you? Pregnant?"

I saw her and Derrek become very uncomfortable, and it hit me.

"Oh, my God." My jaw dropped and my heart skipped a beat. They had talked about eventually getting pregnant, but I was not expecting to accidentally drop their bomb on this trip.

"Oh, my God!" My mother began jumping around and making very high-pitched squealing noises. She grabbed my brother and hugged him so hard; I could see him struggling to take a breath.

I felt awful. Telling your family that you're pregnant is a big deal, and I had just ruined that for them. "Sorry." I mouthed to my brother, who I was fearing was near death from strangulation.

After our psychotic mother let go, and my brother could speak again, he did. "It's cool. We were gonna tell everyone on the trip anyway. Since Steph wasn't going to be drinking."

When someone almost always had a drink in their hand and then suddenly stopped? Yeah, dead giveaway. I reached for Derrek. "Congrats, baby brother."

We hugged.

It was at that point that I realized that I hadn't introduced Ryan yet, except to Derrek and Steph of course. My body was filled with anxiety that I hadn't let Derrek and Steph in on this little ruse I had going on. I would just have to fill them in later. "Guys, this is Ryan, my fiancé." I shot looks at both my brother and his wife, hoping they would get the clue and play along.

Ryan stepped forward with a smile beaming across his face. *Sell it, buddy.* "It's nice to meet all of you." He extended his hand to my mother.

My mother was a hugger. "Oh, we do not shake hands in this family." She pulled him into another death hug.

I continued my glance at my brother, pleading with my eyes.

I got a knowing nod from him. I mean, he knew how crazy our mother could get, especially about my choice to remain single and childless.

After my mother let go, I gestured to my brother. "You already know Derrek and his wife."

"How you doin', man?" Ryan reached out his hand to my brother. "Congrats."

My brother grabbed his hand and smiled with a nod.

My mother went from celebratory to sheer anger. "You two already knew about this?"

Derrek winced and glanced at our mother. "I mean, they work together and hang out. It was only a matter of time before they hooked up." He raised his eyebrows at me.

"Derrek Randall Johnson, don't say hookup." My mother was a very old-fashioned kind of woman. When I was in high school, I merely kissed my boyfriend in front of my mother, and she acted like she walked in on us during the night I lost my virginity.

It made me wonder about our room again. "Why do we have the same room with only one bed," I finally asked. Also giving Derrek a reprieve until the four of us could get together and get our story straight.

"Well, your father and I figure, since there's a ring involved." Mom grabbed my left hand, which of course didn't have a ring on it because, well, we weren't engaged.

Maybe this is the perfect time to back up and explain.

It was about six months ago; I was on the phone with my mother in my condo. Ryan and I had been living together as roommates for about a year. He was watching TV in the living room while I was in the kitchen, trying to convince my mother that my lifestyle was perfectly acceptable.

"Mom, would you leave it alone? I don't care—" I could rarely get an entire sentence out, especially when I was defending my life and choices. I was at a breaking point with her.

"Sweetheart, I want you to be taken care of." Her concern was noted, but not appreciated at this point.

"I can take care of myself. I bought this condo last year, by myself," I reassured her. I knew she just wanted what was best for me. That's why I had a lot of compassion for her, but her way of showing that care has always been destructive. Her priorities were different. I could accept that; she couldn't.

"Exactly, what kind of man will want to marry a woman who owns real estate?" Not sure where her logic came from. At one point, I told her I was thinking about getting a dog and she told me that no man would be interested in a woman with an animal. There was also some weird comment about how animals are not children.

"The kind of man that I would want to marry?" I will admit to my tone being rude. I even saw Ryan cock his head over to see me in the kitchen with a shocked look. Like I said, this conversation needed to end or I was going to say something I would regret, and trust me, I did.

There was silence over the phone until she finally said, "Your life just hasn't started until you have a child." Which, I understood she believed, and I would never take that away from her, but living life with a mother who thought the fact that my show had won Emmys was simply just to tide me over until I found a man, was not an easy task for me.

"Mom, I am living a great life. I have a nice condo, do you even realize what kind of accomplishment it is to own real estate in this area? It's a huge one. I have held Emmys in my hand and been interviewed on the red carpet. I'm doing just fine," I yelled at her.

Ryan turned off the TV and twisted around to watch what was happening in my kitchen. I guess I was more entertaining than his home improvement reality show.

"I just want you to get married so I know you will be safe in that terrible city." Her voice was broken. It was clear she had started crying. She was just so passionate about how she felt a woman's life should go, and it genuinely hurt her that I felt differently. I got that, but what she didn't get was that her acting this way was also hurtful toward me.

I knew I had to do something. "For God's sake, Mom! I'm engaged, okay?" And there it was. The lie of all lies. The thing I said and would regret to the day I stepped on that ship and knew I was going to regret the whole week. I winced as soon as I said it. I knew it was a mistake as the words vomited out of my mouth. My heart was beating so fast.

"What? When did that happen?" My mother was screaming so loud I had to pull my phone away from my ear.

"We got engaged about a week ago, it's still very new." I glanced at Ryan.

His mouth and eyes were wide open. He knew I was digging a very deep hole with my mother. I had told him story after story of how obsessed my mother was with marrying me off and making sure I gave her at least one grandkid.

"Tell me his name!" my mother demanded.

"His name?" I looked at Ryan. I just needed a name, and every name on the planet escaped me. Every name. I don't think I could have remembered mine at that moment.

Ryan began laughing at this point. This was definitely more entertaining than watching some pseudo-celebrities flip homes.

"His name is Ryan," I blurted out in a panic.

Ryan's face fell into one of horror. He wanted to be a spectator in this sitcom trope I had just turned my life into, not be the leading man.

And that's why we are here, on this cruise ship, pretending to be fiancés to save face.

"Lori?" I knew what my mother saw or didn't see on my finger. I wasn't about to buy a fake engagement ring for a trip for which my fiancé and I were just going to break up right after anyway. "Where's your ring?"

I had to think fast. I didn't even know why I wanted to keep up this damn charade. I should have just "broken up" with my "fiancé" before I left for this trip. I wasn't smart enough until just now, to even think about something like *that*.

"Rings are too expensive," Ryan blurted out.

My mother glared at him. "So, you're not willing to put a ring on my baby's finger because you're cheap?"

"No, it wasn't him, Mom. It was me." I needed to save Ryan from my mother's wrath. "I told him that I didn't want a ring."

"But other men won't know you're engaged," she told me. She was very likable, in most situations; she's just old-fashioned.

"Then I will tell them to back off." It was always clear that I was a strong-willed person. I got that from her. We just have different beliefs about things. It's why we butted heads a lot. We were too similar, and I think sometimes it got to both of us.

"You wouldn't have to if you had a ring." My mother was always stuck on those traditions.

"Mom, engagement rings are stupid. The whole wedding industry is a scam. Why make someone feel bad if they can't afford to spend three paychecks on a diamond that was probably mined in an unethical way." I knew it was pissing her off, but honestly, I believed in that idea more than anything. Even if I did find a man I wanted to spend the rest of my life with one day, I would never expect him to pay for some sort of lavish jewelry like that anyway. "Mom, look, I know those traditions are important to you, and I want to honor that, but I just don't agree with you." I gently touched her shoulder.

She looked hurt; I knew she was hurt. I hated hurting her, but sometimes, it was the only way to get my message across. Plus, I was convinced the hurt was centering herself in our fights so everyone felt bad for her and looked at me as the villain.

"Enough of this talk." My father finally decided to say something. He stood from his beach chair and smiled at me. His smile could light up the room. He'd always had a kind soul. I often wondered what kept him married to my mom for so long. He pulled me into a big hug and said, "I'm so happy for you, sweetheart."

The guilt flooded my body. He was happy for me? He was happy about a lie, excited about a lie; he was proud of me because of a lie. I didn't know what to do at that moment, so I sank into his arms. "Thanks, Dad, it's good to see you." After our hug, I looked at my mom. "Both of you."

We might argue, I might not come home much, and we might believe in very different things now that I was an adult with my own thoughts, but I wasn't ready to let go of my parents just yet. I kept holding onto this hope that, one day, Mom would at least accept how I felt, even if she never fully understood.

My dad approached Ryan.

"Sir." Ryan nervously reached out his hand for a shake.

My dad shook his hand with a smile. "You treat her right, okay?"

Ryan smiled. "I have since the day we met." It wasn't a lie, we became fast friends and when I got my job as art director, the only person I knew I could trust to help me with it was Ryan.

I looked around. "Where's Kasey?"

Kasey, my older sister, was also a lot like my mother. She had been determined to land a man and have children like she was racing everyone else. The people she graduated with, me, Derrek, our cousins, everyone. She was the first of us to get married. When her first kid came at twenty, giving up drinking was easy since she couldn't go out and do it yet, legally. So, if she was racing, she'd won. I knew I was okay with coming in dead last; hell I might not finish the race at all.

"The family is on their way. Managing three children is a hassle." My mother always acted like my life was so simple being a child-free adult.

I looked at Ryan. "Note, life is easier without kids," I said passive-aggressively.

My mother simply glared at me as I had just told her that I was evil and planning on destroying the world or something.

"Noted." Ryan was catching on.

"Don't you dare?" My mom's glare moved to Ryan.

"Oh, relax, Mom," I told her. "You know babies have never been in the forecast for me. Besides, don't you have enough love with the three you have?"

"I just want you to be happy." She brushed my hair back behind my ear.

It's the one thing I have never been able to wrap my head around. She couldn't imagine a woman being happy without having children, and I was so desperate for her to get that I was already so happy with my life. Children would only hinder the enjoyment of my life, which I understood was different for her.

"I am happy, very happy." My life felt complete because I was a complete person. I didn't *need* external validation by having a partner or children to feel like a complete person. I was the cool aunt, with the cool job, in Los Angeles. That was enough for me.

"Hey, Kasey!" Derrek called out as my sister and her family approached.

"Auntie Lori!" Becky, my youngest niece came running at me. She was eight, and we had a special bond. I obviously didn't have a favorite, but she was my little buddy. Her long dark brown hair flowed in the wind as she raced toward me and jumped into my arms. She squeezed me so hard; video chatting was never enough for either of us.

I peered over Becky's shoulder and saw her older sister and brother. "Hey, guys."

"Hey, Aunt Lori." Grant, the oldest, was about to turn fourteen, he was the one that my sister was pregnant with before she could go bar hopping.

"Too old to call me Auntie?" Becky had finally let go and I strutted up to him.

"He's a cool teen now," my sister teased. "I'm also not allowed to hug him when I drop him off at school." I looked at my older sister, Kasey. She was always the pretty one. She had this dark silky hair that was always perfect even when she was breastfeeding an infant in the middle of the night. Her smile was infectious. She was also much thinner than I ever was. It was nice when she was pregnant. For the first time, she'd been fatter than me, even if it was because of a baby and not because she was the one with the fat genes. Since then, I had accepted my body as it was, but in my teen and early adult years, I'd hated my size-eighteen figure.

"I wouldn't want to hug you either." I gave her a sly smile. Our childhood was filled with little fights, sometimes big ones, which evolved into us playfully antagonizing each other.

"Oh, shut up." She pulled me into a big hug. "Boy, I've missed you."

"I missed you too." Sometimes, I enjoyed my escape from my family, but other times, I did miss my brother and sister.

A loud horn sounded, and we all knew what that meant, it was time to…

"Time to wave at strangers?" Ryan asked, sarcastically excited.

"You bet! Let's go." We all headed to the edge of the deck. We saw what had to be a thousand people standing on the dock waving.

The next ten minutes were spent waving until all that was left was the open ocean. We were off on our adventure.

"Well, that was fun." Ryan put his arm around my shoulder and pulled me in.

"No reason to be sarcastic," I lectured.

Ryan seemed offended. "I'm not! I may not get why it's a thing, but it was enjoyable." He kissed my forehead.

"Nice, sell it," I whispered to him.

He smiled at me with a sly wink.

"More drinks?" my dad offered.

I nodded. "I'll buy a round." I looked at Grant. "You drinking beer yet?"

He simply shook his head and rolled his eyes.

I chuckled as I headed over to the bar with my sister and brother, who decided to follow me.

CHAPTER 2

LORI

I t was a pleasant afternoon drinking with my family, everyone got to know Ryan, and everyone bought our story. That is, except for Derrek and Steph, who knew who he was.

A gentle tug pulled me away from the rest of the group. "Come with me to get another round?" Derrek directed me away from the rest of the group.

I figured I owed him an explanation. "Sure." I followed him back to the bar.

"Seven perfect margaritas, three Cokes, and a water," my brother blurted to the bartender, then turned to me. "Dish."

I took a deep breath. "Mom was on me, so I lied to her about having a fiancé. I had no idea they were getting these tickets, so I needed to keep the lie going. Please keep this secret. I don't want to have that conversation on this ship."

Derrek chuckled. "I would have already spilled the beans if I wanted to."

I sighed. "Thanks." I shook my head. "I don't even know why I lied."

"Because we have an overbearing mother." Derrek was handed one of the margaritas, and he immediately started drinking it.

I nodded. "Yeah, she's a piece of work." I saw another margarita being left on the bar. I grabbed it and took a sip myself.

"Just so old-fashioned. Her way is the only way. And you are like, anti-mom, so I think you show her the life she could have had."

I shrugged.

"The life she never knew was an option. You intimidate her." It had never occurred to me that I may have intimidated her.

The rest of the drinks arrived. "There's no way we are gonna be able to carry all of this back with us." I gazed around for something to help bring the drinks.

"I can bring them to you," the bartender told us.

We took him up on the offer and headed back to the group with two drinks each.

"Where's the rest?" Dave, my sister's husband, was already pretty drunk.

"The bartender is on his way." Derrek took a sip from his drink and handed the other one to our also pretty tipsy mother.

I looked over toward the pool. "I remember swimming in that pool for hours last time we were on this ship." I wanted to go swimming. I looked at Ryan. "Wanna go for a swim?"

"Hell yeah!" Ryan pulled off the tank top and dropped it near the lounge chair Steph had been resting in.

I had a bikini under my crop top and high-waisted bike shorts. Those too were soon on the ground. We ran and jumped into the pool like a couple of kids.

Ryan came up from under the water totally drenched. "Man, this feels good." Something caught his attention. "What the hell is that?"

I turned around and saw a capsule-looking thing at the edge of the pool. "Oh, that? It's a shower."

"Why?"

"People like to rinse the chlorine off before they get dressed or just head back to their staterooms. I peed in it as a kid." I continued staring at it.

"You what?"

I laughed. "I had met these two kids on the ship, and we were swimming, and I was dared to pee in the shower, instead of the pool. So, I did."

"That's disgusting."

"Ooo, hot guy to your six." I noticed him, shoulder-length sandy hair, and a five-o'clock shadow, he knew how to dress to impress me. He looked like Brad Pitt and both Hemsworths had a baby together.

Ryan turned to look. "Woah, not my type, but I can appreciate."

We were alone, so I felt like we could ogle men together. It felt good to be normal again, for even just a little while.

Suddenly, three familiar voices screamed and jumped in after us. It was my nieces and my nephew.

"Thought you could go swimming without us?" Lilly, the second oldest said as she wiped water away from her eyes and pulled back her mousy brown hair. She was ten and just learned to swim in the deep end.

"I wish this ship had a water slide, like the last one we went on." Grant looked around the pool. As I said, we went on these trips a lot.

I gazed over at Ryan and then behind him to where the hot guy was, but he was gone. I always had this weird fantasy of going on one of these trips and falling madly in love with someone. I wasn't against love, I wasn't even against marriage, it just was never a priority of mine. There was still this part of me that was lonely, and because of my lie, this was not the week I would live out my fantasy. The realization of my lie was just starting to hit me.

"Auntie Lori, let's have a breath-holding contest!" Lilly called out, then turned to Ryan. "How about you, Uncle Ryan?"

Uncle Ryan. That stung. These kids are caught up in all of this too. For the first time, I was thinking it was time to just come clean, and we hadn't even had the muster drill yet. Then it occurred to me, "We should all get out and get ready for the evacuation drill."

Ryan's eyes widened. "Evacuation drill?"

I nodded. "Yeah, it's this thing that they do. We don't actually evacuate, but we get to learn what we need to be doing in case…"

"We hit an iceberg?" Ryan asked sarcastically.

"Well, we are in the Caribbean, so, no icebergs," I countered.

"Pirates." Now he was just being silly.

"Ryan, it's just a precautionary thing that every cruise ship does in case you have to evacuate. It's like when you go skydiving and you have to learn how." I guess I had just been on so many vacations like this, that this just felt normal to me.

"What is the likelihood of a ship sinking these days?" Ryan asked seriously.

I shrugged. "I've never looked it up."

Ryan simply stared at me in utter disbelief. I'm sure to him the idea that I wasn't even nervous freaked him out more.

"It's just a precaution; it's not likely. I've been on plenty of cruises since I was a kid, and I am still fine," I reassured him.

"There are enough lifeboats, right?" He asked sarcastically.

"I think they learned their lesson with the Titanic on that one," I told him.

"We just studied that in school a few weeks ago. Kinda freaked me out," Grant added to the conversation. "That must've been scary 'cause like, you would have probably died." Grant directed his comment to Ryan.

"That's not helping, kid." Ryan splashed some water into Grant's face. They both laughed.

"Guys! We have to get to the muster!" Mom called out to the six of us in the pool.

"Muster?" Ryan looked at me.

"That's what they call the evacuation drill." It was the location you meet on the ship to get ready for evacuation. Each cabin has a muster station where they would meet, which of course had lifeboats. In these situations, we would meet there as if we are going to evacuate, life jackets and all.

"Why didn't you use that name? That name would have freaked me out less," Ryan lectured.

"As if that would have caused less confusion." I lifted myself out of the pool and grabbed a towel. "Let's go," I told him.

The other four followed me and began to towel off. Ryan pointed to the showers. "Do you wanna go use that?"

I peered over there and smiled. "Nah, I don't have to pee right now."

Ryan laughed and shuddered.

We all headed back to our staterooms, which were far from each other. "I think we're all at different muster stations," I said as I was looking over the map.

"Is that bad?" Ryan asked as he changed into a clean outfit.

"Not bad, it's just, there's no cell service out here. So, finding each other if we had to evacuate would be interesting."

"Well, should we consider a muster station of our own? You know? Like, whatever picks us up, we meet at the pool right away, or something?" he asked.

"Not a bad idea. Probably shouldn't be the pool. That would be too crowded. Maybe we just pick a stateroom number and head there. Staterooms are kinda like hotel rooms, they are all numbered pretty similarly."

"So, like, room 1010?" Which was our stateroom number.

I nodded. "Let's bring that up at dinner tonight."

The haunting sound of the emergency alarm even sent shivers up my back. I tossed him his life jacket. "Let's get off the Titanic."

If looks could kill, Ryan would have killed me with that stare. He wrapped his life jacket around his body and fastened it. "So, where all have you been on cruises?" he asked.

"Well, this is my sixth cruise." We headed up the corridor to our muster station as the alarms sounded for the drill. "The first one was an Alaskan cruise, which was super cool. We ported in Vancouver and went up to Alaska that way. That one was a fourteen-day trip."

"How old were you?"

"I was nine. So, while it was fun, it's probably the least fun I've had on a cruise."

Ryan looked confused. "Why was it less fun?"

I shrugged. "All the other cruises we went on, I had a lot more freedom. The next cruise was on this ship, and I was thirteen for that one. I could just grab the key card and tell Mom and Dad I was going for a walk, and they would just say 'bye and be safe.'" When

I was nine, they were a little more concerned about my whereabouts. I was generally stuck in the kid play-area thing all day while my parents spent the day drinking."

"I guess that makes sense."

"So, the next cruise was a Nordic one, it was pretty." We got to the elevator, along with everyone else on our level of the ship. "The fourth one was to celebrate my sister's engagement. That was a Mediterranean Cruise. I was around fifteen then, and I ate so much on that trip."

"Wow, we lived very different lives." Ryan seemed to be enjoying this storytime.

"The fifth one was the one when we went back to Alaska, which was great."

"Was that to celebrate your brother's engagement?" Ryan asked.

"No, that one was to just have a family trip together. Grant was about three for the trip, so it was a different experience."

The doors to the elevator opened and we stepped out to the Promenade Deck. We all stepped out.

"Then, as you know, our last one was on the Great Lakes." I shrugged. "I had no idea those existed, but it was fun.

"You talk about these trips like you do this all the time."

"Maybe we could get some friends together and take an adult trip sometime. Where would you like to cruise?" I asked him.

He shrugged. "I have literally never thought about that."

I bumped into his shoulder. "Start thinking about it. I'm serious."

I realized that this was weird for him, but I wanted to make it better. He stayed pretty silent the rest of the muster. Afterward, it was time to get ready for dinner. Dinners on cruises were either formal or semi-formal. This one was semi-formal since it was our first night on the ship.

I slipped into my little black dress. Ryan was still very quiet.

"You, okay?" I asked.

Ryan nodded. "It's just, we grew up so differently, that's all."

"So, why are you being weird about it?"

Ryan turned to me with a smile. "Sorry, I don't mean to be. It's just, I feel uncomfortable here. It's seriously not you or your family, it's just here." He grabbed a blue necktie and draped it over his white button-up.

"That makes two of us. But for me, it's my family." I knew we needed to get down there. "Sorry, I gotta get my makeup done." I slipped into the bathroom and grabbed my makeup bag from under the sink. "Trust me, you'll get used to being on the ship in a few days." I looked over the lipstick options I had brought with me and asked, "Hey, what color lips tonight?"

"Go with that maroon. You always look hot in that!" he called back.

After we were ready, my hair loosely curled and of course the maroon lips, we headed out to the restaurant for dinner with the family.

The restaurant was dark and very fancy. One large table contained my whole crazy brood. "Hey, everyone."

"Hello, sweetheart." My mother stood and gave me a hug. "I ordered you a zinfandel." Mother knew me well.

Ryan and I sat down in the two empty seats at the table. I gazed over the menu. "Everything looks so good."

"Holy shit, I've never had lobster." Ryan was practically drooling.

I smiled at him. "Have it. It looks amazing."

"Want a bite?" he offered.

"Would you like a bite of the prime rib?" Prime rib has always been my favorite, especially on vacation.

His questioning look told me he was picky about his prime rib. "How do you take it?"

"Mooing." I always loved steak as raw as the government would allow. Maybe one day I would die from E. coli, but I don't care so much when steak cooked raw tastes so good.

"Maybe a little bite." He put his face right next to mine. He was good at selling this fake engagement. He reached his lips to mine and gave me a little kiss on the lips.

"Ewww!" All three kids hated the sight of me kissing a boy.

I turned to Steph and peered down to her stomach. "Hey, little one, you ewwing in there too?"

Everyone laughed.

It was a pleasant evening. We laughed, ate, and drank. It was like a happy family gathering. Until my mom decided to start digging like she always did.

"So, when are you two gonna give me my fifth grandchild?" She took a sip of her rose wine.

"We haven't even set a date, Mom; we have no idea when kids are happening." I tried to keep my cool. I was not going to ruin the evening for everyone else with a fight with my mom.

Mom's face lit up brighter than I had ever seen before. "When?"

Don't start, I thought to myself, my eyes gently closed. I could feel my hand clenching. I felt the gentle touch of Ryan's hand on my shoulder.

"We aren't sure if kids are in our future." Ryan seemed to be taking the brunt of all my mother's rage.

I looked at him. "Right, we are just both so busy. Honestly, it would be so unfair of us to have a child."

"Well, that's why you stop working when you decide to have children." My mother was such a proponent of stay-at-home motherhood. It worked for her, it worked for my sister, it worked for many women in America and all around the world, but it wouldn't work for me.

"My career is my child." Which had become true to me. It took up so much of my free time, and I wouldn't have it any other way. "Besides, there are so many families in this country who can't live on one income."

"Well, a career is not a child." My mother was offended. I get it. It probably wasn't the correct thing to say to her.

"Look, Mom, I know that," I started. "It's just, for you and for Kasey, having children was the ultimate life goal. For me, it's different. I want to do other things with my life, like travel, have a great career, and win awards, that kind of thing."

"That's quite selfish."

"I'm selfish?" I was very offended.

"Lori." I knew Ryan wanted me to stop and just take the hit. He didn't want an explosion in the middle of this fancy restaurant.

"No, Ryan." I pushed him away. "She's the selfish one," I blurted out.

"How exactly am I being selfish? I put my life on hold for all of you," my mother contended.

"Because you keep projecting your life onto everyone else." My voice was so loud, it was starting to attract the glances of everyone around us. "You think that every girl needs to want one hundred children and be a stay-at-home mom and get married to the best guy in the world." I darted from my seat. "For your information, I don't need or want any of that. I want a career, travel, friends; I want a life and that life doesn't include children, and that's okay!" I was able to stop myself before I ruined my entire ruse.

My mother looked around. She was embarrassed. "You are making fools of us. Sit down and stop acting like a three-year-old." But not embarrassed for the right reasons.

"No, I don't think I will." I reached into my purse and grabbed some cash and threw it on the table. "I need to get out of here." I felt the tears flowing from my eyes now. I turned and hurried out of the restaurant as quickly as I could. I was embarrassed that I had let my emotions get the best of me. I needed alcohol quickly. I knew there was a bar not too far, so I dashed that way as quickly as I could.

CHAPTER 3

RYAN

As Lori ran out of the restaurant, I turned to her mother, since the fight happened anyway. "You know, she told me horror stories about you. I wanted to give you the benefit of the doubt that she was overreacting. But you know what, you're the selfish one. You can't even be proud that your daughter won an Emmy. You can't be proud that she has made great strides in her career and is a very well-respected art director. Have you even come to see where she works? How she works? No. Wanna know how I know that? I'm one of her animators, and she is the best boss I could ever ask for." I tried to keep my voice down, but everyone was already looking. I saw staff beginning to surround our table.

"Is there anything we can help with?" The host asked as he approached our table in his penguin suit.

"No, my fiancée and I are leaving," I told him, locking eyes on Lori's mother.

I rushed out the door and saw her about a hundred feet ahead of me. "Lori! Wait!" I called out, trying to catch up.

She stopped and turned to me, her eyes red and puffy. She had been crying so hard, her face still red from yelling. I pulled her into my arms. I loved her. She was like a sister to me, and I was never going to let anyone treat her like that again. "What can I do for you?" I squeezed her tighter.

She burrowed her face into my chest. So much so that my shirt was becoming wet with her tears. "I just want a drink… or six," she mumbled.

"You got it. Drinks are on me." I looked in the direction of the restaurant in hopes that someone from her family had followed, but no one came after us. This was just proof that she was alone in her world. No, she had me, and thankfully, that seemed to be enough, most of the time.

"I just want her to be proud of me." She looked up at me.

Those words pierced my heart a little. "They are proud of you, Lori." I hadn't ever seen this side of her, but I also hadn't seen her around her family either.

Lori was always such a businessperson; it took hanging out with her and watching her go through her last break-up to see an emotional side of her.

We had gone out for drinks—me, her, and a bunch of the other crew. It was to celebrate our big win at the Emmys. She was the last to arrive, and we had all decided that she wasn't paying for a single drink all night. She was late, and her live-in boyfriend was supposed to join us. When she arrived alone, she looked a little disheveled.

"You, okay?" I asked her as I stood.

"Luke …" She was just staring into space.

"What about him?" I had honestly thought the worst. Like, he was in a car accident and was in the hospital, or he had just been diagnosed with something awful.

"I went home to get changed, and I heard noises from our bedroom. I headed that way, and there he was. With another woman." Tears formed in her eyes.

"What do you mean with another woman?" I asked.

"I mean *with* her, Ryan." She sat down, still seeming to be in shock.

That night became about drowning her sorrows. She threatened to throw away her entire bed as she began drinking and then followed through the next day. She had called in sick and tossed her entire bed, frame and all, into the trash. She went out and immediately bought all new things. Luke was also kicked out that day. Last I heard, he ended up dating the girl he was with for a while, until she found him in the arms of yet another woman. He's an urban myth in our office these days. New animators come in and hear whispers of the man that made Lori cry. Like I said, she doesn't cry that often, so when the newbies hear about it, they mostly don't believe it.

I walked with my arm around her shoulder until we reached the bar she had been heading to. We sat down, and I called the bartender over. My eyes couldn't believe what I saw standing in front of me.

"How ya going?" It was the hot guy we saw by the pool, and he was Australian. I peered over at Lori since she had always said she was obsessed with the Australian accent.

"Someone's having a rough night." I motioned toward Lori.

"Sorry to hear that. What can I get ya?" He leaned over the bar closer to Lori.

She looked up at him and smiled. "Can I get a Cosmopolitan?"

"Absolutely." He turned to me. "And you, mate?"

I thought about it for a moment. "You know, surprise me with a good beer that's not too hoppy." I usually enjoyed letting bartenders pick my beer, especially if I was somewhere I've never been before.

"You got it." He turned away from us to get our drinks.

I poked Lori. "Hey, make yourself feel better, flirt with him," I urged her.

She looked at me. "I'm engaged, remember?" She was mocking herself.

"Well, as your fiancé, I say go for it."

She shook her head. "I'd rather just drink tonight." She sounded so defeated, I wanted her to be better.

The bartender returned with our drinks. "There you go, guys." He slid the cosmopolitan toward Lori.

"Where are you from, if I can ask." I knew Lori wasn't going to get to know him, so I decided to help her out a bit.

"Australia, born and raised in Melbourne." He seemed so proud of it.

"What brought you here?" I continued to ask.

"This ship used to cruise around Australia, New Zealand, and Papua New Guinea, so I got a job. Then the ship was traded to the Caribbean, and I decided to stay with it." He looked around. "I'll check back in with ya later. I got other people to serve." He walked away and began serving others.

I looked at Lori and realized that this was bothering her. "Hey, you're gonna be alright."

"They just make me feel so insecure about everything. I'm such a failure to them, especially my mother."

"You're not a failure though. You're a very successful person," I tried to reassure her.

She shook her head. "But not to them. I'm never gonna be enough for my family."

"Why do you want to be enough for them? You're you, not them." She always seemed so free from her family, but seeing this side of her opened my eyes. She was just a sad little girl who wanted validation from her mom. Where was my hero?

"Everyone wants to be accepted by their family, me included." She wiped her tears from her face and drank her cosmopolitan. "I just want to get drunk tonight."

I smiled and nodded. "Okay then, let's do it. Well, you do it. I think it's best that one of us stays sober enough to not fall into the ocean."

Lori gave me a little chuckle. "Yeah, you're right, thanks for being here for me."

"Any day, you know that." I pulled her into a big hug. I wanted to take all her pain away. I knew I couldn't do that; I knew that the hot Australian bartender couldn't do that. The only person that could fix Lori's heart, outside of Lori herself, was her mother.

"Done with that drink, bartender!" she called out.

The bartender came back to her with a smile. "Hey, you ready for another cosmopolitan?"

Lori nodded. "Yeah, get me another one." She slid the empty glass back toward the bartender. "What's your name?"

Maybe she was getting loose enough to start flirting. It would be a nice ego boost for her to flirt with the hot Australian. No one else on the ship was going to care if we were flirting and yet "engaged." Just as long as her family didn't see, I kept a lookout for her, just in case.

"My name is Justin," he answered and pointed to his name tag.

"Kid, I worked retail before I made it in animation. I never look at nametags anymore." That was always one of her biggest complaints. She hated when people would look at her nametag and use her name. She said it was always the people that looked down on her for being in retail.

Justin laughed. "Well, it is weird when complete strangers know your name." He grabbed the glass. "I'll get you another drink alright?"

"I still think he's hot," she told me as she watched him walk away.

"Are you going after him?" I asked her.

"It's probably not the best idea for me to 'go after him'," she mentioned. "I mean, someone in my family could see it, and that would be bad. I just don't wanna add to the drama." She was right. It probably wasn't the best idea to have her hitting on someone so close to where her parents currently were, especially when they knew she was upset.

"Okay okay, so you're letting the Aussie go," I said just as he returned to the bar.

"What was that, mate?" My heart sank. "Did ya need something?"

"We were talking about your accent. She loves Australian accents." I tried to cover it up. My air was ripped from me as Lori's elbow connected with my gut.

"Ryan." Lori grabbed her drink and began to down it. "This is a great Cosmo," she said through slurred speech. She had already had drinks over dinner, was downing more, and tended to be pretty lightweight with alcohol, she was already buzzed at this point.

After a couple more drinks, she was drunk and feeling a lot better. "Man, my parents suck; they really do." She placed yet another drink down on the bar. "Justin!" she called out.

Justin approached us. "You may wanna take your missus home. She's pissed."

"Damn right, I'm pissed, Justin. My parents are terrible people. What do you call a terrible person in Australian?" She was slurring her words.

"She's pissed in both versions of the word," I joked.

"We call them wankers," Justin answered.

"Well, my parents, my sister, her husband, my brother, and his wife are all wankers." Her eyes were opening and closing very slowly. "And for the record, I'm no one's 'missus.'" She pointed directly at him.

"Oh, I thought you two were together." He looked at me questioningly.

"It's a long story, but no, we're not together, mostly 'cause we're both into men." I laughed uncomfortably.

"Oh, well, maybe you'll pop by sometime this week and tell me the whole story." He seemed relieved that she wasn't with someone.

The gears started to turn in my head. Maybe this week was about finding her a fling to feel better. It had been a while since she hooked up with anyone. "We will absolutely stop by again. You work tomorrow night?" I wanted him to make sure I understood he was interested in her, and not me, so I peered over to my drunk best friend.

Justin shook his head, "I get tomorrow off."

"Maybe we'll see you again tomorrow then." I stood from my barstool and held onto Lori. She was fall-over drunk and I wasn't sure if she could sit on the barstool by herself.

"Maybe tomorrow I can get to know her sober." Justin looked quite concerned for Lori as she smiled at Justin.

"You're hot," she blurted out, followed by kissy faces.

"Thanks, mate." He smiled and walked to the other side of the bar after giving me back my card that I had handed him earlier to create our tab.

"Come on, drunkie, let's get back to the stateroom and sleep off the rest of this night."

CHAPTER 4

RYAN

The next morning, I woke up in bed with a woman, which is very unlike me. You know, it's those nights when a girl gets super drunk, you take her home, undress her, put her in her pajamas, and hope she doesn't barf all over everything.

I felt bad for Lori, her family was mostly horrible. She'd always said she was the black sheep of the family. I guess I never realized just what that meant until I saw the fight that happened last night.

I slightly opened my eyes; the sun made it a little harder to open them fully. I had a weird sensation of moving but everything around me seemed stable. It was the first time I felt the ship sway like that. I sat up and placed my feet on the floor. I felt dizzy. "Well, that's not cool."

I hadn't drank enough to be hungover. Maybe this is what sea sickness was. I didn't like it. I decided coffee sounded like a good idea, so I made my way over to the coffee pot and began brewing it. I peered out the balcony door. The ocean was gleaming from the sun rising above it. Never had this been something I would have experienced. I grew up in Brooklyn, and not in a rich family. Our idea of a family outing was camping in the Hudson Valley. I remember once, we had a road trip up to Maine, it was my favorite vacation.

"I smell coffee." It was the muffled sound of my best friend rising from the dead.

"You want some?" I asked.

"Not sure yet." She had to be very hungover. She got more drunk last night than I had seen in a while, and she didn't sound great.

"How long have you been awake?" I sat down on the bed and looked at Lori.

"For like, a minute."

"How hungover are you?"

I just heard a groan coming from under the covers, and that was all I needed.

"Want me to run and see if they have something?" I leaned forward to the dresser and grabbed some clothes.

"It's more than just a hangover."

"When does the sea sickness go away?" I grabbed the swim trunks I had been wearing yesterday and tossed them into my suitcase.

Lori sat up in the bed and looked at me. "It's different for every-one. When you're also hungover, it takes a little longer." She didn't seem as dark as the last time I had to be her caretaker because she'd drowned her sorrows in alcohol. Her breakup was clearly worse than this.

She scared me back then. It was before we were as close as we were now. It was the reason we became roommates. She would come into the office, and she just wasn't herself. When we started working on our show, she was always the life of the office. She would bring donuts nearly every morning for the team. She was bubbly, but not the annoying kind. When she got cheated on and broke up with her ex-boyfriend, she became dark and dreary. We all missed her. So, I started taking care of her. I wanted to make sure she was okay; I wasn't sure if she had an advocate.

I think she appreciated the fact that I would just check in with her every morning, and ask her how she was. Pretty soon, she started inviting me over for movie nights, where she would just sit with me and cry, while we watched some "chick-flick" as she always called them. After a few months of that, we started going out for drinks and food. Eventually, she was back to who she always was. A couple of months after she bought her place, she asked if I wanted to rent her second room. We've been best friends ever since.

"And yes, I would appreciate you getting something from a shop to help fix this." She smiled. "I'll be out on the balcony getting some fresh air." She rolled out of bed and reached for the dresser. "Oh, God." Lori fell to the floor holding her stomach.

I got dressed. "I'll go see if they have a convenience store and ask for the best anti-nausea pill they have."

Lori looked up at me. "Sounds great." She went to the bathroom. I knew she was going to throw up, and I didn't want to hear it, otherwise, I was going down with her.

I hurried out the door and missed the puking. I had gotten to the elevator when the seasickness truly got to me. "Woah." I nearly fell over from the dizziness that just wouldn't go away. I did stumble but managed to stay on my feet. *Don't throw up... don't throw up... don't throw up...* I kept thinking to myself as the elevator made its way down. The doors opened, and I walked out into the plaza of the ship. I looked around, hoping to see something that had a sign out front that said, "Hey, you, with sea sickness, come in here." Unfortunately, that wasn't going to happen for me.

"Come on," I whispered to myself.

It got the attention of someone nearby. "Seasick?"

I turned to the voice; he was a scrawny little guy wearing a uniform. "You have no idea."

He smiled and pointed up the stairs. "Head up there, to the left. You'll see a little convenience store and they have everything you can get over the counter in there."

"Hey, thanks." I smiled.

I made my way up the stairs and saw the convenience store. "Thank God." I was still feeling like I was going to die, and climbing stairs did not help, even in the slightest. I entered the store and walked right up to the counter. "My friend and I have the worst seasickness, plus my friend is hungover, what can we do about that?"

The guy laughed. "You're a bit later than our normal rush on day one at sea." I was about to purposely barf right on the counter. He must have noticed my irritation. "Dramamine is what you want." He grabbed a bottle and handed it to me. "You should have taken this before you got on the ship, but it'll still do the trick."

I took it from him. "Thank you."

I returned to the elevator, I still felt sick, but I was hoping that this stuff would kick in soon. My stomach started to rumble again. "Oh boy." I managed to hold it in all the way up to my floor. "What is it about that elevator?" I turned to look at my enemy, then stumbled my way down the hallway until I got to our room. Upon opening the door, I asked, "Is there still coffee?"

Lori poked her head through the balcony door. "I'm still on my first cup." She was smiling through her nausea.

I walked over to the balcony door. "You look like you're feeling better."

She shook her head and held out her hand. "I feel like death. I'm just good at hiding it."

"What? I'm supposed to tip you too?"

"Shut the fuck up and give me the drugs." She grabbed the bag from my hands and took a few of the pills. "Please, God, give me peace from how I feel!" It was good to see her joking again.

"We're at sea all day, right?"

Lori nodded. "Yeah." She plopped down on the chair and looked over the ocean. "We land in Jamaica tomorrow morning."

I moved to the other chair. "What's there to do in Jamaica?"

"There's this great place, called Dunn's River, where you can climb a waterfall." She seemed excited about it.

To be honest, it sounded amazing. "Cool, did you wanna do that tomorrow?" I wanted to try to get everything off her mind. The more I could keep her away from her family, the better.

She nodded. "I loved it last time we did it."

I had never thought I would want to climb a waterfall. "Cool, done." That's when I realized, "Shit, I forgot to get the coffee."

Lori laughed. "Sorry, I distracted you!"

I shook my head and flew back into the stateroom for some

much-needed caffeine. I was already starting to feel better. This medication was doing the trick. That or it was simply just a placebo, but either way, I didn't want to throw up as bad.

I grabbed a mug and poured the black liquid that I saw as heaven in a cup. I needed this coffee. I have always been one of those people that take their coffee as black as it brews. Lori constantly made fun of me for it. Then again, she made fun of herself, saying that she wanted some coffee with her morning milk. I sauntered back out to the balcony and carefully lowered myself to the chair, seeing as how I had a hot cup of coffee in my hands. "Thanks for inviting me."

"You're the one saving me," She told me. "We just gotta keep this up for seven days; then we can magically break up by Christmas." After a sip of her coffee, she asked, "How's your bitter, burnt water?" She smirked at me.

I took a sip. "Utterly delicious." As I said, she likes to make fun of my coffee habits. "You sound like last night didn't upset you too much."

She groaned. "I was hoping that was some drink-induced dream." I knew she was kidding. "For real, it sucks, but I think it was something that needed to happen, but I suppose not around my nieces and nephew."

I nodded in agreement. "I mean, you needed to put your mom where she kind of belongs." I wasn't a fan of her mom when she told me stories, but now, man. "She has no right to tell you how you live your life."

Lori painfully smiled at me. "I mean, she's still my mom, and she thinks she knows what's best for me."

"Yeah, well, that's 'cause she doesn't know you. She sees you as a person with a uterus, and your only job is to cook children."

Lori gazed out onto the ocean. "Because that's what *she* did, and it's the correct way of life."

"But you're not that person."

Lori looked at me, deeply. "Is there something wrong with me that I'm not?" Was she kidding?

"No, there's nothing wrong with you!" I couldn't believe she started thinking that. Her mother had beaten her down enough that she was questioning herself. "You are just fine the way you are!"

She simply shrugged as she gazed out at the vast ocean.

Me bringing this up had only brought her back to her darkness. My stomach rumbled. "Wanna get some breakfast? I'm finally hungry." The pills had officially set in for me, so they had to have been working at least a bit for her.

Lori stood up. "Let's see what I can hold down. I think there's a buffet on the Promenade Deck." She clearly wasn't feeling better just yet.

I rose and smiled. "Let's do it."

We made our way down the corridor. Being on a cruise ship was an unreal experience. My body was aware that the ship was moving while my brain attempted to maintain stability. My body and brain were no longer communicating. I now understood what people meant by "sea legs" and couldn't wait to have them.

We entered the same elevator, which had almost been covered in my insides. "Good memories."

Lori cocked her eyebrow at me.

"Inside joke…"

"With who?"

"Myself?"

Lori laughed, rolled her eyes, and shook her head. "Good lord, Ryan."

The elevator door, or as they call them on cruise ships, lift door, opened to the promenade deck.

"Let's see if we can avoid my *entire* family." She laughed as we made our way to the Vista Café, which was where breakfast was served. "I want pancakes." She sounded like she was a drug addict looking for her next hit.

I laughed. "You should never *actually* get pregnant. You get some crazy cravings without it." She did. There was one time, early in our friendship when we ordered a pizza. It was pepperoni, extra sauce, and four cheese, and Lori looked at me and said, "I'm gonna get some chocolate sauce." It was a craving she had. She needed to put chocolate on her pizza.

"Is it that weird to crave pancakes for breakfast?" she asked.

I shook my head. "It's not the desire. It was how you said it."

She jumped in front of me. "Sometimes, I just need a freaking pancake, okay?" Which didn't help her not to sound like she was a drug addict.

"Okay, get yourself a pancake and put some chocolate on it," I joked.

"Chocolate chip pancakes are a thing, loser." She always got defensive when I made fun of her for her weird mixing of foods.

"Uh-huh." I just wanted to take her mind off last night as much as possible, except maybe one thing. "You remember that hot Aussie bartender?"

Lori stared into space. "Vaguely." Her glance returned to me "Did I flirt? I can't flirt when I'm drunk."

I shook my head. "I wouldn't call what you did, flirting."

She cupped her face in her hands. "Oh, God…"

I chuckled. "It wasn't that bad, Lori."

"We are going back to that bar tonight to apologize," she commanded.

"You asked him if he worked tonight…" I reminded her.

She looked at me, seemingly trying to think back to the night before. "I did?"

"You did. He doesn't."

She panicked a little. "Why did you let me talk?"

"It wasn't that bad; he took it very well. And I'm sure he gets it all the time; I was the only mostly sober person there."

"Promise?" she pleaded.

We entered the Vista Café and saw all the food. "Woah."

"I smell pancakes." And that was it. I lost her. She was off, looking for her pancakes.

I looked around, not even sure where to start. "Eggs," I said to myself as I walked toward all the food.

I found the egg cooking area, and there was a chef standing behind the counter. "What kind of eggs would you like?" His Jamaican accent was very thick.

I smiled. "Over easy, please."

He nodded and got right to work on my eggs.

I gazed around to figure out if I wanted anything else, and I realized the perfect thing to harass my best friend even more. "Hey, question."

"Yes?"

"Where are the waffles?" I smirked.

"They're over around the corner." He pointed to the left of the counter he was at.

"Perfect, thanks!" I couldn't contain my stupid excitement over the thought of her face when I walked up to our table with a plate of waffles.

My eggs were done after a few minutes, and the cook handed me a plate with two perfectly cooked over-easy eggs. "Those look great," I complimented.

"Thank you, enjoy your waffles." The cook smiled.

I journeyed over to where fresh waffles were poured onto a plate sitting under a warmer light, "Those look so good." I grabbed a plate and grabbed two hot fresh waffles. I slid my egg over the top of the waffles and ditched my egg plate. I love the taste of loose yoke on bread.

After a little more exploring, I found some bacon and sausage, I grabbed a bit of both, then turned another corner and found some fruit and grabbed a bowl. "Syrup." I looked around.

"Over in the center." A woman with stringy hair and a screaming baby in her arms pointed to a kiosk.

"Thanks." At least I knew I didn't have to tip her, though maybe I should have, she needed a little extra for having to put up with a screaming baby.

I got myself some good old maple syrup, my favorite. That's when I noticed the coffee bar. "Yes, more coffee." I looked down. "Except, my hands are full." I gazed around the loud dining room and found Lori already sitting at a table by the window. I made my way through the crowd to her. "Hey." I plopped my waffles down on the table.

"Sure, waffles." She shook her head, expression filled with disappointment as she looked at my plate.

"Bigger than your sad-ass pancakes," I shot back. "More coffee?" I pointed to the kiosk with the coffee bar.

"Yes, please. Two creams and some sugar," she begged.

I shook my head in the same disappointment as I walked away from the table.

"Grab me some water, too, please!"

I raised my hand with a thumbs-up letting her know that I heard her.

I grabbed two cups of coffee and a glass of water, then returned to the table and placed the creams and sugar in front of her. "I can't defile coffee," I told her.

She rolled her eyes at me, most people thought we were annoying as hell. Most people also mistook us for married. I guess choosing me as her fake fiancé was perfect.

I sat down and immediately broke the yoke, mixing it with the syrup. "So, what do you wanna do today?" I took a big bite of waffle dipped in my delicious mixture.

"Not watch you eat." She hated runny yoke. I couldn't understand why; it was absolutely delicious. "Seriously though, I'm thinking of just a day out at the pool. Some relaxing swimming, sitting in the hot tub, reading on a chair, and day drinking." She got quiet for a moment, then asked, "Would you mind if I just chill by myself?"

I nodded. "Of course, I'll find something else to do. This ship is just a huge city on water, so, hey." I was a little disappointed, but I understood that she wanted to just escape and be by herself.

"Are you pissed?"

"Not even a little. I'm disappointed, but we have six more days to hang out. You do some self-care today," I reassured her.

She nodded with a tear in her eye. "Thanks, I just want to be alone."

"I get it." I got up and walked over to her. I wrapped my arms around her from the back. "I love you, Lori." I kissed the side of her head. I just didn't want this week to suck for her.

CHAPTER 5
LORI

This trip had started out miserably, and I just needed some relaxation and to forget the night before, which I couldn't remember much anyway. Today was better. Ryan got me medication and then we had breakfast. Later, I got ready for my relaxing day, alone.

I had my blue bikini on and was headed to the pool. In my bag, I brought a book, some suntan lotion, and my credit card for a cold drink. It was about to be the best few hours of my life.

Once I reached the pool, I saw my brother Derrek sitting alone at the bar. I wanted to avoid him, go sit in that vacant lounge chair I could see in the distance, and drink alone. "Hey, Derrek." I knew I was going to talk to him. We had been so close when I still lived in Minnesota, and I missed him more than anyone else in my family.

"Hey, about last night," he responded.

I shook my head. "Let's not talk about it." It was the last thing I wanted him to mention. I gazed over my shoulder to see the lone chair had been taken. I sighed and plopped my bag on the bar. The book fell out slightly as the bag tipped to one side.

"Go read your book." He looked down at it, disappointed.

"Why are you alone?" I asked.

Derrek shrugged. "Kind of the reason I wanted to talk about last night."

That got my attention. "Okay." I slid onto the barstool next to my brother. "Talk."

Derrek looked at me, then down to his drink. "Steph and I got into a massive fight last night after we all left the restaurant," he began. "You started something."

"I didn't mean to." I felt bad that I had created so much stress that Steph and Derrek had a fight.

Derrek had tears in his eyes when our gazes met. "It was a fight that needed to happen."

"Derrek, what's wrong?" My concern for my brother grew. I wanted to know what was making him so upset.

Derrek was silent for a few minutes. "Have you ever felt like you've made a huge mistake?"

This was not what a big sister wanted to hear when the conversation started with an argument with his wife. "What do you mean?"

"I mean, have you ever felt like you made a huge mistake, and you choose to continue that mistake every day of your life?" He took a big gulp of his beer.

Now I was getting pissed. "Derrek, you better be talking about buying a house, because you can't be talking about your marriage or that baby she's gonna have."

Derrek looked at me. "I love Steph, and I'm thrilled to be having a baby." He went silent again.

"But..." I knew there had to be an addition to that sentence. "Are you not happy?" I needed to know what was going on with my little brother.

Derrek shook his head. "I don't know." He took another drink from his beer. "I think it's just I didn't explore my feelings enough." He continued to be cryptic.

"What feelings?"

"Never mind."

"No, not 'never mind'. What are you talking about?"

Derrek finished his beer and placed some cash on the counter. "There should be enough there to buy you a drink; have at it." With that, he walked away.

Now I wanted to get to the bottom of this, but how? I watched as he walked away. I wanted to follow him, but I knew he would tell me what he wanted to tell me in his time. I figured I should get Steph's side of whatever happened, so I headed toward their stateroom.

I moved my way down the corridor, still feeling a little sick from the ship moving. I reached Derrek and Steph's door and knocked, hoping Derrek hadn't come back here. He would know exactly why I was hanging around.

The door opened, and Steph was standing on the other side, her face was red and puffy from crying. "Hey."

"Steph, what's going on?" I figured she wouldn't hide anything from me.

She fully opened the door, letting me in. "Balcony."

"Sounds good." I headed out to the balcony and waited.

Steph joined me after a few minutes with some coffee. "I can't have a lot of caffeine right now, so, decaf, sorry." She handed me a mug.

I took it with a smile. "That's fine, thanks."

She sat down next to me. "I'm afraid my marriage might be over." She was trying to keep it together, but I saw some tears falling.

"After one fight?" I took a sip from the mug, realizing she didn't know I knew.

Steph leaned forward, her elbows on her knees, and her mug in her hands. Her eyes peered over the water. "I've known since we got together, but he loved me, so I went with it."

"What are you talking about?"

Steph turned to me. "Really? I figured you wouldn't be that ignorant. Your brother likes men."

I *did* know, to an extent. He had never truly come out to me about his sexuality, because it didn't matter. Whoever he chose to love, I would love with my whole heart. I looked at Steph. "But, he loves you."

Steph cocked her head. "Sexuality is fluid; you know that."

"So, you talked about this?" I wanted to know everything.

"I take it you already talked to him, and he didn't tell you much." She looked out over the ocean again; it was bare and vast.

I nodded. "Yeah."

"Well, don't tell him I told you anything." She took a sip of her coffee.

"No, of course not." I leaned over to match her posture. "What did you guys talk about in your fight?"

"We talked about the fact that he fell in love with me, and I was the only girl he was ever attracted to." She took another sip of her coffee. "He was happy he fell in love with a girl, because he wasn't sure how your parents would react to a son that was attracted to other boys."

"They aren't that bad." I hated defending my parents, especially my mother. I knew she would feel weird about it, but at the end of the day, they would accept him for who he is, and they would love whoever he brought home with him.

"Well, when you are the kid facing it, I'm guessing it's a little scarier," Steph mentioned.

I nodded. "I guess you're right." I placed my hand on her back. "You, okay?"

"Not really." She sat back and placed her hand on her stomach. "I just didn't think I'd raise this kid as a single mom." She laughed through some tears. "Then again, I guess I asked for it, marrying someone I knew was more attracted to men than me, but when you get married, it means you don't want anyone else." I think she was more or less talking to herself at this point.

"The argument couldn't have been that bad," I reassured her. "He does love you."

Steph looked at me. "What did he say to you?"

"He just said that I caused your argument."

She shook her head. "What a dick. No, you didn't cause the argument." She took another sip of her coffee. "This argument has been building." She stopped and looked guilty.

"Steph, what?" I inquired.

"I knew our marriage was failing, I just didn't want to be a statistic." Now she was the one being cryptic.

"Your point?"

"I got pregnant."

I was shocked. "Wait, are you telling me that you got pregnant to trap him in a marriage that neither of you are happy in?" I couldn't believe what I was hearing. Everyone knows things like that never work.

She looked down at the floor of the balcony. "It's not my proudest decision. And don't get me wrong, I wanted to have a baby, and I will love this kid so much. I don't want you to think that I regret getting pregnant. It's just, the idea that he would feel obligated to stay was a plus."

I wasn't sure how I felt about any of this. This child was already going to be living in a broken home. I loved Steph, but I respected her less now. I wanted them to be happy, but I don't think they would be together. "How long have you two been feeling like this?"

"Truthfully, the whole marriage. I would say, I started feeling unhappy when he stopped feeling fulfilled, which was about a year ago," she explained.

I didn't know what to do for her. I didn't know what she should do.

"I just don't want to be a statistic," she moaned as she leaned back in her chair.

That statement always pissed me off. "Come on, Steph! Divorce is a real factor. Do you want your child to be raised in a family that isn't happy?"

Steph looked at me. "You don't get it. You're not married, Lori!" She was now also pissed off.

If the idea of not being a statistic was enough to piss me off, imagine how I felt when someone said I don't get it because I don't have something they have. I have never been ignorant about life. "This has nothing to do with it being different when you're married. Believe it or not, divorce is sometimes the right answer."

"Do you even know how much it costs to get divorced? How much is involved? The fact that I don't need to have the word divorcee behind my name."

"See? That's what I'm talking about. Before that last sentence, I was behind you on reasons to not get divorced, but simply not wanting to because you don't want to be labeled as a divorcee or a single mother? That's the worst reason to stay married." I wanted her to see the truth. If she wasn't happy, then she needed to walk away. "Other than vanity reasons, is your marriage worth saving? Do you even love him anymore?" I was worried about asking the next question. "Did you just want kids?"

"No," is all she responded with.

"No? To which one?"

"I don't know," she started. "Of course, I love him. I never stopped loving him." Her gaze shifted toward the sky. "I just wanted to believe it was forever, but it's not," she explained. "I know that. I just wanted to do what I could to keep him around, so no, I didn't just want kids." She looked at me again. "I just..." She wiped a tear from her eye.

"Are you afraid that you'll never find anyone again?" I wanted her to see that she was the one being naïve about marriage.

"Kind of," she admitted. "No one ever wanted to marry me. They just wanted me for a good night. Now, I'll have the extra baggage of a divorce and a kid. Can't imagine anyone wants to date that. Your brother was the only man that ever cared about me. If we got married, then he never had to come out to your parents, and I got what I wanted, too, for the most part. Then something about this trip set him off."

That's when it hit me. "Oh, my God."

CHAPTER 6

RYAN

Lori needed to have a day by herself, so I decided to explore the ship. There was still so much that I hadn't seen yet. I had heard there was even a casino on board. Not that I wanted to gamble, but I wanted to see what this ship had to offer, and if some money ended up on a blackjack table, well damn.

I came across what appeared to be a club level. It had an auditorium, and a couple of lounges, and there it was that casino. "Blackjack," I said to myself as I made my way into the hot smelly casino.

I gazed at the older people playing slots as I worked my way through the crowd. People-watching while they're gambling is one of my favorite things to do. People are so focused on that jackpot they'll never get, people getting something and acting like they just won the lottery, and people losing everything and beginning to cry. Call me an asshole all you want, anyone who gets so into gambling is a fool. It was why I had to help pay rent for a few years as a teenager. My dad was a gambling addict and sent us so far into debt we could barely stay afloat for a few years. I always vowed to stay away from it, but I enjoy gambling. The difference between me and my dad was that I knew I was going to lose, and if I won it was a great perk.

"Ryan?" Derrek approached me with a half smile.

"Hey, man!" I held out my hand for one of those manly high-five handshake things.

He tossed his hand against mine. "What are you doing here?"

I nodded to the blackjack tables. "Thought I'd throw some money away with some twenty-one. Wanna join me?"

He nodded. "It'll hopefully get my mind off of… things…"

"Your sister is at the pool trying to feel better about the blow-up last night." Just in case he knew how to make her feel better about blow-ups with their mother.

"Yeah, I saw her, and she's not what I'm upset about." He seemed uncomfortable as he placed his hands in his pockets and couldn't make eye contact with me.

I reached my hand out and placed it on his shoulder as I smiled, "Wanna waste money with me?"

He looked at my hand and returned my grin, "I'd love to waste money with you."

"Cool, let's go." I led him to a blackjack table that had two empty seats, "You played this before?"

"Not once," he whispered.

I looked around. No one else at the table seemed to hear him. "Okay, you wanna get as close to twenty-one as you can," I whispered back. "If you don't like your hand, hit; if you do, stand." It was the easiest way to explain the game very quickly. I placed fifty dollars on the table and looked at Derrek.

"Right." He reached into his wallet and threw another fifty on the table.

The dealer, with a sour look on his face, dealt out cards to those in front of him.

My cards were an eight and a three. I tapped the table, and the dealer tossed me a seven. I waved my hand to let him know that I was staying.

Derrek had been watching what was going on as everyone else at the table created their hands. He also tapped the table and was tossed a jack. "Ten?" he whispered to me while pointing at the jack.

I subtly nodded.

He waved his hand the same way I did.

"Winner." The dealer pointed toward Derrek.

He laughed with utter delight as he saw the chips move toward him. "Cool." It's not the best way to play blackjack for the first time ever. It's generally better when you lose miserably the first time.

"You've at least gambled before, right?" I whispered.

"Just slots." He wasn't as quiet.

I nodded. "Alright, that's good enough."

"What? You think I'll get addicted, or something?" He laughed.

I shrugged. "It happens." I looked at him. *Damn, I wish he wasn't straight… and married.* I had always been attracted to Derrek, but he'd always been with Steph.

"You still in, Sonny?" The dealer looked at me.

"Yeah sorry." I pulled out the rest of my cash. "Can I just cash all of this in for chips?" I wanted to spend some more time here.

The dealer nodded and exchanged the remaining $50 for chips.

I looked at Derrek and smiled. "I'm coming for you."

Derrek smiled, with a slight blush. "I'd like to see you try."

We played a little more blackjack. I won a couple of hands, and Derrek won a couple of hands, but at the end of everything, I lost all the $100 that I had left in cash.

Derrek and I left the casino laughing hysterically. "That was a blast!" Derrek said as we entered the Coral Lounge for a drink.

We sat down at the bar. I bit my bottom lip as I questioned whether or not I should ask him about what he was so upset about. His mind was not on it, so why bring it up? Instead, I turned to the bartender. "Hey barkeep, how about two martinis, on me."

"Thanks." Derrek looked around the lounge. "Man, this is a nice place."

"Way different than your average sports bar," I added.

"A lot quieter and better smelling than that casino too." He squished his face as he recalled how disgusting the casino smelled.

It did smell. Smelled like smoke and body odor. I was happy to be out of there. "Hey, what time is it?"

The bartender delivered our drinks. "It's 2:30."

I turned to Derrek. "More quality time." I smiled. The realization hit me like a ton of bricks. I was flirting with a married man. Not only a married man but a straight married man. "I mean, 'cause we never get to see each other."

"Right." He had a hint of disappointment in his voice.

"To our great vacation. It may have started like shit, but it's gonna be great!" I raised my glass for a toast.

Derrek raised his glass and clinked it with mine. "And to new beginnings."

"New beginnings?" He brought it up; I was just double-checking.

Derrek took a big drink and turned away from me. "Just wanting to start over with something in my life. Something that I may regret." He turned back and glanced at me.

I didn't want another member of that family to be all depressed and abandon me. "Your sister and I are gonna go climb Dunn's River when we get to Jamaica. Did you wanna join us?" I blurted out. "I mean, obviously Steph can't go, so I get it if you can't."

"I'd love to." His smile was so cute.

"Good." I was looking forward to spending more time with him when we landed and got out on the island. "Is there anything you wanna do on the island?"

He nodded. "I just wanna go hiking in general. The river, through the rainforest, the beach."

"When do we head out again?"

"We have most of tomorrow on shore. I think we leave at like 5:00 or something." He scrambled around his wallet. "I'd have to look at the itinerary to know for sure."

"It doesn't matter." I placed my hand on top of his to stop him from looking for the itinerary. "We'll have to figure it out before we get off the ship tomorrow morning. For now, let's just enjoy each other's company." I was hoping to get him to tell me why he was so down.

"Why aren't you wasting your day away with my sister?" He took another gulp of his martini.

"She wanted to be alone. The fight last night upset her," I explained. I could only imagine what she went through when she was a kid and teenager growing up in that house. A crazy mother whose only idea of life is becoming a mother if you have a uterus. I had no idea how they would feel if we ever told Lori's parents the truth about who I'm attracted to.

"Yeah, we haven't had a blowup like that since Lori decided she wanted to move out to Los Angeles. When she decided to go to the California Institute of Arts my mother went crazy."

I had never heard stories like this and wanted to know more. "What was her problem with Lori going to one of the best schools for what she wanted to do?"

"Well, I remember her saying that she didn't want to be nearly two thousand miles away from her future grandchildren and that the Twin Cities was a perfect place to raise children." Derrek took another drink. "And to make matters worse, my parents never supported Lori in her dreams of one day running the animation department of the Walt Disney Studios."

That was both of our dreams when we met. One would have thought we would be rivals, but she had become one of my closest friends in the years I worked with, and now, for her. "So, going to California was nothing but bad news."

Derrek nodded. "Yeah, I mean, I was going to miss her, but I also knew she was sure what she wanted, and she was determined to get it."

I took one final drink out of my martini. "What should we do now? I kinda wanna discover the ship."

"Okay, I know there's a show in the auditorium. I think it's a magic show. Wanna go?" Derrek jumped off his barstool.

I nodded. "A magic show sounds awful, but let's do it." I followed him out of the lounge, and we made our way to the auditorium. "Looks like they start seating in twenty minutes. Wanna get another drink?" I pointed back toward the lounge.

He shook his head. "Nah, we could just stick around here and chat."

I nodded. "Alright, sounds good." There were still things I didn't know about him. "So, anything you wanna talk about?" I decided to pry just a little to try to get him to talk.

"I think I'm getting divorced when we get home." There it was. The bomb was dropped and my heart sank.

"Wait, what?" I asked.

"We haven't been happy for a while; I thought a baby might help. The baby was a huge surprise, but I was kind of relieved when she said she was pregnant, thinking things would get better." He looked down at his feet. "It didn't."

"I'm so sorry." I pulled him into a hug.

"It's okay. We just wanna try and make it easy. Even though the baby isn't here yet, we wanna make things easy for him." He pulled away from my hug and looked guilty.

"It's a boy?" They hadn't said they knew the sex of the baby.

Derrek nodded, still looking down at the floor. His guilt was almost palpable. I wanted to do something for him. Divorce is never easy. I experienced it as a kid, and I wouldn't wish what I experienced on anyone. Custody battles, a lot of yelling, judges asking me who I wanted to be with, counselors visiting me and grading my parents, it was an awful experience. "I just hope it's amicable."

Derrek nodded. "It is. We want to still be partners when it comes to the baby, we just don't want to be together anymore." He finally looked at me. "It's the best choice; it just still hurts."

I smiled. "Right, I'm sorry."

"I don't make her happy, and neither of us feels fulfilled in this relationship."

I sat down on a free chair. "You always seemed to be so in love."

"I mean, it sucks. I love her, I do. But it's not fair to her to stay in a marriage when I think I might want something different." He collapsed into another empty chair.

"Are you into another woman?" It never occurred to me that their possible divorce could be from an affair, physical or emotional.

"No, I'm not." He looked at me, the silence was deafening for the next few moments. "I just think I jumped into marriage so quickly. She was the first girlfriend I ever had. I fell quickly and thought that's just what you did. You dated, fell in love, and got married. That's the way it goes." He looked so hopeless.

"So, you got married to appease your mother." I knew that story very well, considering the fact that I was on a ship pretending to be his sister's fiancé to appease her mother.

Derrek laughed and nodded. "That may have been a huge reason why I felt like I needed to jump into marriage." He looked up at the ceiling. "I mean, like I said, I love her. I just, I think I feel…"

"Unsatisfied?"

"Yeah, I just feel kind of trapped, you know?" I could see him beginning to tear up.

"Sorry, did you wanna talk about something else?" I leaned in toward him.

"No, I feel like I need to talk about this, I need to hear everything out loud." He looked at me questioningly. "You ever feel that way? Needing to talk about your issues out loud, so that you know if you sound like a complete idiot?"

I nodded. "Of course, sometimes even just talking to yourself helps with that."

Derrek became uncomfortable. "Sorry, I can take a hint."

"Oh God, no, that's definitely not what I meant!" I reassured him. "I mean, that's what I do."

Derrek seemed relieved. "Oh, good. I thought I was annoying you."

I shook my head. "No, of course not." I touched his hand. "I want to hear about your problems."

Our faces were so close, I could feel his breath. I wanted to kiss him. I had this thought that maybe the *something different* he wanted was me.

The doors to the auditorium opened.

"I guess they're seating now." My eyes locked with his.

"Yup. That twenty minutes flew by." He rose from his seat and headed toward the auditorium.

I sighed and followed him into the hall for the magic show.

The magic show was awful, but all magic shows are. Lori loved them. She watched that one reality show, which she often corrected me on that it's more like a gameshow than it is a reality show. She watched it every week throughout its season. I'd often hear her yelling, about how the trick works and how that trick was so cool. I just didn't get why people were into magic. I found it silly. To make it worse, this particular show was a comedy and magic routine. It wasn't funny.

I would peer over at Derrek every time the climax of a trick would happen, and he was smiling ear to ear. *Another Lori,* I thought to myself when I would see that big doofy smile. I couldn't start having feelings for him. I had to keep reminding myself that he was married. Even if that marriage was ending soon, he was still straight.

After the show, we exited the auditorium and Derrek looked at his watch. "Hey, look at that, it's just about 4:00." He looked off into the distance. "We need to face another family dinner."

I nodded. "Let's do it." We started walking in the way of my stateroom.

We got there and found Lori looking out the sliding glass door. She turned around and saw Derrek. "Hey." Her tone seemed sad, and then she ran over to him to pull him into a big hug.

Derrek and I exchanged looks. Both of us were confused. "You okay, Lori?"

Tears now in her eyes, she looked up at Derrek. "I'm fine." She straightened out his hair. "How are you?"

"I'm fine." His confusion was obvious.

"Are you ready to face the family again?" I broke into the conversation.

Lori looked at me, cocked her head, and rolled her eyes. "Can't you just go and say I was lost at sea?"

I shook my head. "Nope, you are going to be a big girl and face your mother. This time, maybe stick to water."

"Oh please, I am already pretty buzzed from my day drinking."

She walked over to the closet where she had unloaded her formal wear. "Maybe this?" She pulled out a blue dress.

"It's great," Derrek told her. "I better head back to my room to change. I'll catch you two at dinner."

I turned to Derrek and stopped him at the door. "It's going to be okay," I told him.

He nodded. "I know."

CHAPTER 7
LORI

stuffed myself in the blue dress and watched as Ryan strutted out of the bathroom. "The last time I dressed this nice two nights in a row was… never."

I chuckled. "It's ship life."

"Are you feeling better?" Ryan placed a hand on my shoulder.

I was, but I was also worried about the rest of this week. With Derrek and Steph's drama, the worry of my mother realizing I lied to her doubled. I worried that everything was just going to implode. "Just sad for Derrek and Steph." I was sure the two had talked about it.

"Yeah, that makes sense. I wonder when they'll tell your parents," Ryan mentioned.

"I'm curious about that too." I walked up to the bed and grabbed my purse. "Plus, this Christmas is going to be weird since he'll be divorced from his real wife and I'm breaking up with my fake fiancé sometime before then." I realized that I couldn't do that to my mother. I was going to have to marry Ryan for real at this point.

Ryan let out a little chuckle. "Let's go." He reached out his hand for mine. "It may look best if we walk into dinner hand in hand."

I grabbed his hand. It had been gnawing at me all day. Was my brother attracted to Ryan? They had spent a considerable amount of time together today, and I was hoping that maybe Derrek had said something, or something maybe could have happened. "So, what did you two talk about?"

Ryan shuffled around on his feet uncomfortably. "Not a lot, just that he was planning on getting divorced and wanted to start over and find something more satisfying."

"Did he say what would be more satisfying? He didn't tell me much about what was happening." I hated that I was being so nosey, but he was my baby brother. I was very protective of him.

Ryan shook his head. "Nope."

We got to the restaurant and found my family. You could cut the tension with a knife as we approached the table.

I stood at the table and took a deep breath. I guess I was going to be the first to try to make this right. "First, I would like to apologize to everyone about how last night turned out. It wasn't one of my finest moments." I glanced down at my mother, whom I made eye contact with, hoping she would also be an adult and apologize.

My mother's snooty attitude didn't change. "I accept your apology."

I was very close to starting another fight. "I'm sure we all said things and did things we're not proud of." I looked at her again.

"Please, let's just have a nice evening." It was clear my mother had no intention of apologizing, ever. I sat down and kept my gaze on her. I was disappointed, but then again, I shouldn't be. She was never one to accept her responsibility for actions, especially when it came to fights with her children. She always had the mentality that she gave us life and provided for us, so in the end, we owed her something.

I turned to Ryan. "I want wine."

Ryan rolled his eyes. "Then order some." His look was very judgmental.

I knew he thought it was a bad idea for me to drink, but sometimes, that's the only way I can handle my family.

The server came by our table. "Can I get you started with some drinks?"

"Where are you from?" My father inquired. My dad was the

quietest one in our family. He often sat back and listened. He was also very hands-off with child-rearing. Growing up in my family was like the 1950s, but we had a color television, internet, and phones in our pockets. They were the stereotypical nuclear family with antiquated gender roles.

"I'm from Liverpool, England," the server answered.

"Your accent seems different from normal English accents." My father wasn't great with words. Sometimes he came off as ignorant in the most abrasive way.

"There are like forty different accents in the UK, Dad," I whispered, hoping he wasn't offending our server.

"She's right. The ones more Americans are familiar with are the ones around London." He grabbed out his notebook. "I am from up in the northern part of the country." He readied himself to write down our orders "Now, what can I get you?"

He was good. He knew how to change the subject without getting angry. I wish I did.

"Whatever red wine you have," I told him.

"Do you prefer more of a dry red or a sweeter red?" he asked.

"Dry." I just wanted wine. I wanted something to numb the irritation I had toward my mother who was too damn proud to apologize for being a bitch the night before.

Everyone else ordered, and the server dashed off to the bar to get everyone's orders in.

I looked at my father. "Seriously? You barely open your mouth all trip so far and you criticize someone on his accent?"

"Lori, we are having a good dinner. We don't need any of your attitude tonight." My mother scolded me like I was still a ten-year-old child while she looked over her menu.

I felt Ryan's hand on my knee, and he squeezed. "Relax," he whispered.

I took a deep breath and looked at him. "Thanks."

He nodded with a smile, then grabbed his menu and perused it. "You know what I want? A burger."

Becky let out a laugh.

I wasn't sure what was so funny about Ryan wanting a burger. "What's so funny, you silly girl?"

"We are on a ship with all kinds of cool foods, and you're gonna get the most basic thing on the menu?"

"Sweetie, we don't judge others for what they want to eat," Kasey whispered to her. My sister was incredible with her kids. She was doing her best to raise her kids to be kind and compassionate toward other people. I remember my parents complaining about people all the time when I was little. She was trying to be better than that.

"Sorry, Uncle Ryan," she said as she slid down in her chair, embarrassed.

"It's okay, kiddo," Ryan answered back with a smile. "I like your dress."

Becky perked up and grabbed her kids' menu. "Thanks, I picked it out myself."

"It was a very good choice." I joined in the conversation.

Becky smiled bigger and sat back up in her chair like she had been before.

Maybe this dinner wouldn't be so bad if I focused on the people that I wanted to be around. Which was not my parents.

Dinner went well. We ordered our food and managed to have civil conversations all night. Even between me and my mother, until—

"So…" My mother poked at the remaining couple bites of her cheesecake. "When are you two planning on getting married?"

I looked at Ryan. "We haven't set a date yet." This was not going to end well.

"Well, you had better." She looked at me. "You're not getting any younger. You're nearly thirty and your eggs are drying up." There it was, always back to the baby talk. No matter how many times I had told her since I started puberty that I had no interest in having kids, she always expected me to change my mind.

"Kids aren't even on the radar for us," Ryan interjected.

My mother looked at him with obvious disgust and disappointment. "You're to do your duty as a husband and should very well want children."

"Why?" I asked. "Isn't it okay for him and me to want to see the world?"

"You can see the world and still have children. We took you on incredible vacations like this one," my mother argued.

"Neither of us wants kids," I told her.

"Do you want children, Ryan?" my mother asked.

He shrugged. "I guess, I always figured if I ended up with someone that wanted kids, I would have kids, and if I ended up with someone that didn't, I would be okay with that too."

"See, you're driving him away already." My mother clearly didn't hear what Ryan said.

"With all due respect, Leslie, your daughter isn't driving me away. You're driving her away," Ryan told her sternly.

"Excuse me, young man, you're not part of this family yet, so you can't say things like that."

"I think I can. I've known Lori for years, and I have only heard horror stories about you and your attempts at controlling her life and uterus. She doesn't want kids, and I'm okay with that."

It felt good to have Ryan stand up for me. That was exactly the kind of man I wanted in my life when I did find the right guy. Someone who didn't care that I would be fine living as a couple for our whole lives and would stand up to my mother for being the bitch she was. "Look, you, Kasey, and now Steph all wanted motherhood. I don't."

"Then this boy must not be right." My mother never had any sort of tact.

"Mom!" I expressed embarrassment. "You have no right to say something like that."

"The right man would make you want to have children," she told me.

"Again, with all due respect, that's not how it always works. I will not sit here and let you insult me," Ryan told her.

"My daughter deserves to be a mother." I knew it was a passion for my mother. It was something that filled her life with such joy. To raise three kids and be a stay-at-home mom. She couldn't look past herself enough to see that other people had different priorities and desires in life.

"You have three grandchildren and one on the way already, and that's amazing. I don't need children to be happy, Mom." I was basically pleading with her to see my perspective. I knew it was futile, but I still hoped.

"I told you that I wanted a nice dinner and here you are starting a fight again," she blurted out.

I was dumbfounded. Even when she started the conversation and she was the one insulting Ryan, I was the one starting the fight?

"Mom, you started this one," Derrek jumped in. "You have never respected Lori's choices, not when she wanted to be an animator, not when she decided to move to LA to pursue that dream, and not when she has told you a thousand times that kids won't make her happy." He stood. "You owe her and Ryan an apology."

"I am not the one who started this. She is the one who doesn't respect my wishes for her to be happy."

"I am happy, Mom. I live in a great condo; I have a great-paying job; I have amazing friends." I realized fighting with her was fighting with a brick wall and I needed to be done. "I've never been happier," I told her.

Ryan pulled me in for a hug and kissed the side of my head.

"I just want to go to bed," I thought out loud. I stood and made my way toward the exit.

Ryan followed me and grabbed my hand. "I'm sorry."

"Two nights in a row. What are the rest going to look like?" I asked.

We made our way back to the stateroom, and I walked out onto the balcony. I hated this. I hated how much I resented my mother, and I hated how much she clearly resented me. "I just wish I was normal."

"No, don't do that," Ryan said as he followed me onto the balcony. "Normal is a setting on a washing machine. You are who you are, and that's okay." He grabbed my shoulders and looked at me. "She is who she is, and that's also *mostly* okay. It's okay until she makes you feel like this."

"It sucks to resent my mother," I told him.

"I know." He pulled me into a hug.

I let go and slipped back into the stateroom to grab a sweater. "It's a little chilly out there tonight." Once back out to the balcony and asked, "Can I be alone for a little while?" It was always my MO to retreat and shut down when I felt like this. I liked being alone with my thoughts. I needed to calm down; I needed to rest; I needed to make sure I didn't have a panic attack.

"You got it. I'll be right inside, in case you change your mind." He kissed my forehead.

I rested my arms on the railing of the balcony and looked at the moon and its reflection in the water. I resented my mother, but at this point, I also resented myself. I sometimes wished I was that person that wanted kids. All of my friends either had already had them or were just starting to have them. I saw how happy they were. I went to their sex-reveal parties and rolled my eyes at them. I wished I could get excited about the idea, but I just didn't have that maternal gene. It wasn't easy being someone in her late twenties that didn't want kids. I felt judged every day. It was ten times worse. I sat on the lounge chair and cried.

CHAPTER 8

RYAN

The next morning, I woke up feeling better, at least I didn't want to die. "I guess I have what they call 'sea legs.'" I whispered to myself as I peered out the balcony door. The sun was rising, and I already saw Lori taking in the view. The smell of fresh coffee gave me an early morning rush. "How long has she been up?"

I crawled out of the most comfortable bed I have ever slept in and followed the smell of coffee. I poured myself a cup and joined Lori outside, "What time is it?"

Without a word, Lori shrugged.

"Lori, you okay?"

She shook her head.

I grabbed her and pulled her in for a hug.

"It was all just a lot simpler when I was thirteen being stuck on a boat with my family." She told me as tears started to well up in her eyes.

I hated how much she was hurting. Two nights in a row with her mother being an absolute terror. I didn't know how to help her. I didn't know what was going to make this week okay. There was no turning back now, we were trapped on this ship with her family.

Just then there was a knock at the door.

"I'll see who it is." I gently patted her on the shoulder and made my way through the stateroom. On the other side of the door, I found Kasey. "Hey."

"Hey, is my sister up?" she asked.

I nodded and pointed to the balcony.

"Great." She pushed past me and hurried her way to Lori. "Hey."

"What do you want?" Lori's tone was harsh.

"I'm sorry for the way Mom was last night," Kasey said as she leaned over the railing to match Lori's pose.

"It sucks, Kasey." The tears Lori had been fighting back with me a minute ago were now streaming down her face.

"Yeah, I've never understood why every choice you make is the wrong one to Mom." Kasey was always the mom growing up. According to the stories, Lori would tell me, her mom was so busy trying to be the perfect housewife she forgot to raise her kids in the process. Their family seemed more dysfunctional than mine and that's saying something considering my dad up and left when I was sixteen because his gambling sent us so far into debt, and my mother is still working toward getting herself back upright.

"I don't get it either. I'm happy, I'm successful, I love my life." Lori continued to feel like she needed to defend her entire existence.

"Then why do you let Mom get to you?" Kasey asked bluntly.

Lori shrugged. "I guess it's because I still desperately want to hear her say that she's proud of what I've accomplished in my life. But it's just never good enough."

"To her, a working woman is…"

Lori cut Kasey off. "A failure."

"Wait, seriously?" I didn't want them to know that I was listening in, but I had to understand this woman's mentality.

Lori turned to me. "Our mom looks at a working woman like an old maid. Someone not worth a man choosing her as a wife."

"Your mom truly is stuck in the past, isn't she?" I was astounded. I never thought people like Leslie still existed, clearly, I was wrong.

"You still want to join this family?" Kasey was half joking. She was still oblivious to who I *really* was, which was good.

I chuckled and nodded. "Yeah, I'm good."

Lori even let out a chuckle.

"So, I guess we are doing a group thing after lunch on the beach." Kasey finally dropped the bomb.

"Great, more time with a woman who hates me," Lori blurted out.

"Lori, that's not fair. She doesn't hate you. She genuinely thinks she's doing what's right for you," Kasey argued back. I couldn't believe she had the audacity to still defend their mother. No wonder Lori felt so alone with her family.

"Yeah, well, you popped out a kid at twenty, so Mom left you alone," Lori told her. "You don't know what I go through." She paused. "And then Derrek doesn't know what I go through because he was the boy, the baby, the one that didn't have to use a uterus to provide her grandchildren."

"No, but Steph heard it from her too. I remember one time, Mom was complaining that those two had been married for three years and weren't pregnant yet. She was disappointed in Steph for that one," Kasey told us. "Anyway, I just wanted to check in on you. Did you two want to have breakfast with us today?"

I nodded. "That sounds nice."

"We're getting ready now, so meet us in our stateroom in an hour?"

"An hour?" It only takes me about twenty minutes to get ready for something fancy.

"We have three kids; it takes some time to get ready." Kasey laughed.

After breakfast, Lori and I were back in the stateroom. "So, what should we wear to this Dunn's River excursion?" I asked.

"Swim gear and water shoes." Lori was feeling less depressed after spending some time with her nieces and nephew.

"What the hell are water shoes?" I asked.

Lori walked up to the dresser and opened her top drawer. She pulled out a pair of shoes and showed them to me. "These are water shoes." They were black and looked skintight.

"I don't have those." I had no idea what kinds of things I should have packed for a trip like this. The most exciting journey I went on was the cross-country road trip I did when I moved to California.

"That's fine, I'm sure a store on the ship has a pair, we can stop there and see." She grabbed a one-piece swimsuit out of the same drawer.

I was startled by a knock at the door. "Got it," I told her as I opened it to find Derrek. "Hey."

"What's up? How's Lori?" he asked.

"I'm fine. You two don't have to take turns checking in on me. It was just another fight with Mom. God knows we have had hundreds and we will have hundreds more until I have officially hit menopause." Lori closed the door behind her to change.

"I see she's passed the depression stage and right on to angry."

I nodded.

"What's the plan? Do you two have one?" Derrek asked.

"The three of us are gonna climb that waterfall and then I guess meet with the family at one of the beaches." I was worried about hours with her family, but maybe the sun's rays might kill whatever demon lived in Lori's mom.

Lori glided out of the bathroom in a blue one-piece swimsuit. "You wanna go with us up Dunn's River?"

"That was the plan if that's cool with you," he answered.

Lori nodded with a sweet smile and patted her brother on the shoulder. "Then maybe you can tell me what's going on." She kissed him on the cheek and walked over to her suitcase. She pulled out another bag and stuffed it with a towel, those swim shoes she mentioned, and sunscreen.

"What do you mean?" It was clear that she and Derrek were going to dance around this secret Derrek was trying to hold tight.

"Let's get going." I wanted to make sure there was no rift between Lori and the only member of her family that doesn't make her crazy. That was my job, after all, to stop Lori from having any family drama, which I was clearly failing at. I also wanted to make sure Derrek was okay.

"I wanna get my trunks on. How about you guys meet me at my stateroom in like twenty minutes?" Derrek started to make his way to the door.

"Sounds good," Lori said as Derrek walked out.

"Okay, I think I am ready to climb a waterfall." I realized how crazy that sounded.

CHAPTER 9

LORI

We met my brother at his stateroom. I fussed with the strap of my swimsuit as I knocked on the door.

Steph greeted us with a simple "Hey." It was awkward, to say the least.

"Derrek is coming with us." I gazed down at my feet. "Did you wanna join us at the beach later?"

"Nah, I'm feeling sick right now." She shot a look at Ryan. "You three have fun." She then glared in my direction with the same fierceness.

I realized what she was assuming. Ryan and Derrek hung out, which clearly meant something happened. I pulled her a few feet away. "Nothing happened between them. Ryan would have told me," I whispered. I was hoping that would give her some sense of relief that she wasn't also dealing with that.

Steph shook her head. "Maybe not yet, but it will." Tears formed in her eyes as she shuffled her feet. "I realized it last time we were out in LA."

"What?" I hadn't noticed anything.

"They are very attracted to each other." Her tone was harsh as if I should have seen it too.

As far as I ever knew, my brother was married and in love with

Steph. It never occurred to me that anything else was an option. "Steph, I don't think …" I was cut off by her walking away.

Steph made her way back to the door and called out to my brother, "Derrek, your sister and friend are here." She turned back to the door and looked at me as if I did this to her as if I knew all along and brought Ryan on the trip to break them up. She slammed the door.

"Well, she's a joy right now." Ryan walked up and grabbed my shoulders.

"It's fine." I pulled away. It was. I understood that she was pregnant, hormonal, having marriage issues, and realizing that her husband wanted to leave her. This was going to get complicated.

The door opened revealing my brother now wearing his orange swim trunks with cream-colored palm trees and a matching solid cream button-up that hung open, "Hey, guys." He seemed sad. "That's the first time she's talked to me since this morning."

I felt bad. I hated that he was having such a miserable time. I pulled him into another hug. "I love you." I wanted him to know that I was on his side. I would back him and no one else. I just wish I knew what was holding him back from being honest with me. I knew he needed to tell me in his time, but it hurt to know that I wasn't someone he felt safe with yet.

He hugged back hard; he slightly trembled in our embrace. He was holding back from crying. "Thanks, I love you too."

Only a mere ten minutes later, we stepped on land; it was wonderful to be on firm ground again. I loved the way the ship felt, but I needed stability, and if I was only going to get that from standing on dry land again, so be it.

"Sweet, sweet earth." Ryan held out his hands as if he was praising the ground he was walking on.

"We didn't leave earth, you bozo." I laughed at his ridiculousness.

He turned to me. "I mean earth, like land, dirt under my feet!"

"Let's get to Dunn's River." I laughed and pushed him.

"How do we get there?" Ryan looked around.

"There's gotta be a bus." I walked up to an information booth. "I mean, it's a tourist trap. So, there's gotta be an easy way to get there."

"We could call a cab," Derrek offered.

I nodded. "That's another option." I grabbed a brochure. "Hey, look at this. We do have a bus." I shrugged. "Well, a shuttle. And it shows up every half hour."

"Perfect," Ryan said as he walked up to me.

Derrek looked at his watch. "We have about ten minutes to get to the stop. Where's it at?"

"Shouldn't be far." I looked around and saw a bunch of tourists congregating around a large sign. "That looks promising." I guided our group down the street to what appeared to be at least *a* stop if not *the* stop. "Shouldn't take us more than ten minutes to walk that."

We arrived at the stop just as a white shuttle with a blue stripe across it parked at the curb. "Perfect timing," Ryan blurted out as he hurried to the shuttle.

We boarded the vehicle and managed to find three seats near each other. "I'm excited." I hadn't done this for years, and I couldn't wait to do it again. I remembered being thirteen and thinking how cool it was that I was climbing a waterfall. Our parents cheered us on from a distance as the three of us helped each other climb. Things were a lot simpler then.

I gazed at all the beautiful scenery as we rode past. I had a lot of time to think. If my brother did like Ryan, and Ryan liked him in return, why shouldn't they be together? I glanced at them. They were talking and seemed to enjoy each other's company. I made the decision that I was going to get these two together. How perfect would it be to have them fall in love on this trip? I guess I was going to play matchmaker for the rest of the week. Deciding to hookup my fake fiancé and my married brother was going to be a complicated mess, but what in this family wasn't? I could think of better people to hookup, but I was going to make this happen.

"What's going on in that head of yours?" Derrek leaned up against me. He was always concerned about my well-being. Out of my two siblings, he was always the one that understood how much my mental health dips when I spend too much time with our mother.

I looked at him. "Just taking in the scenery." I smiled. "Love you, baby brother."

"You sure that's all?" He wrapped his arms around me and squeezed. The kindness in his voice always made me feel safe. My brother was my safe space growing up. I just wondered why I wasn't his anymore.

"I guess. I'm just sad for you. I want you to be happy, and you're not," I told him.

He smiled at me. "I love you for that, but this is for the best," he said. "I am already happier knowing that this is going to be over soon."

"I'm glad." I reciprocated the hug. "If there's anything you wanna tell me, I want you to know, you can." I wanted to make sure all doors were open for him to tell me what I so desperately wanted him to tell me.

"I'll keep that in mind." He was clearly planning to continue to be in the closet with me.

We made it to Dunn's River. We stepped back out into the hot and humid air of Jamaica. It was both wonderful and torture.

"Lori!" Ryan exclaimed in a hurried whisper as he nudged me in the side with his elbow.

"Ow, what?" I asked.

"Isn't that the hot Australian bartender you were trying to flirt with on the first night?" He gestured to a group of people that were getting off a different shuttle.

I looked over and saw his shoulder-length wavy blond hair. He nonchalantly put it behind his ear. He straightened out the tropical loose button-up that he wore. It was totally him.

Our eyes met.

"Shit." I looked away.

"He's on his way," Ryan told me.

"Hey." That Aussie accent already had me weak at the knees. I have always been a serious sucker for that accent.

I knew I needed to make eye contact so as to not give away how mortified I was about our last interaction, but I knew if I looked him directly in the eyes I would probably turn to stone. "Hey."

"You're the girl from the other night." He smiled. "How was that hangover the next morning?" He chuckled.

I was totally mortified now. "Nice to see you again." I didn't remember a whole lot from that night, but his looks, *that* I remembered.

"Justin, right?" Ryan asked.

He laughed. "Yeah, that's right."

"Sorry, this is Derrek, my brother." I grabbed onto Derrek's arm so strongly, I am honestly surprised he didn't say anything. I was so nervous. "Derrek, this is a bartender from a bar near the restaurant we ate at on night one."

"Nice to meet you." They shook hands. "So, you got shore leave?"

"Oh yeah, we always do. I have to be back on pretty much after this to start my shift, but at least I get a little fun shore time," he explained.

"Are you here with other bartenders?"

Justin shook his head. "No, just me. The others all wanted to do other things. They've all done this. It's my first time here, so I wanted to take it in."

"Why not join our party?" Ryan asked as he winked at Derrek.

"If that's cool, sure. I gotta think this is more fun to do with other people," Justin told us.

"Yeah, that sounds great." I glared at Ryan. What was he doing? Was he playing matchmaker? Were Justin and I his little project? How dare he play matchmaker with me when my plan was to play matchmaker with him!

The four of us headed down the walkway toward the stairs leading to the bottom of the falls. There were street merchants on either side of the walkway. Some that were wrapping hair, others that were sitting on blankets trying to sell little trinkets. It was so fun to see. I was stopped by a lady who asked if I wanted to get my hair wrapped. I turned to her and said, "No, thank you." And we continued on our way.

We made our way down the stairs, and off in the distance, we could see people climbing the falls.

"This looks so cool." Justin seemed very excited.

I thought it was cute that he was so excited to try this. He looked like I probably did my first time too. I couldn't get my mind off of how sexy he was. I wanted him, but how would that even work? I was here with my fiancé after all. We got to the bottom of the stairs and made our way into the crystal-clear water.

"Wow, this is amazing. I don't think I've ever seen water this clear before," Ryan said to everyone.

"Welcome to the Caribbean, mate. You ever been before?" Justin asked.

Ryan shook his head. "I haven't even been off the mainland US." He then took a quick dive into the water. "This feels so good."

We started our journey up the falls. It was a very subtle incline, which is what made it safe to climb by yourself. We had declined a guide. Since there were so many people going up, we felt safe enough.

I had brought a waterproof camera with me since I didn't want to chance losing my phone in the water. "Hey, wait, let's get a before picture," I asked the guys.

"Sure, I can take it for you." Justin reached for the camera in his hands when Ryan stopped him.

"No, man, you gotta be in the picture with us. We're a group here." He grabbed the camera and turned it to take a selfie.

We all got close and smiled.

I felt Justin's fit body against me. He felt warm and made me quiver at the fantasy I was starting to have of him and me hooking up. I heard the click of the camera, and everyone let go of each other. I hadn't felt this way for a long time. That way you feel when you *really* like someone. The butterflies you get whenever they look at you, or the way your heart races when you feel their touch. I felt that way now. It had been over a year since my last breakup, and simple hookups with some regular fuck buddies didn't give me the same rush that Justin did. This was dangerous territory.

We continued to climb moss-covered rocks. I nearly slipped a few times, and once on purpose. It was Justin that kept catching me. We stopped at a pooling of water on the falls.

"Let's take a break," Derrek called out as he swam around in the pool of water.

Ryan joined him and the two started a water fight.

That's when I saw it, a spark. I finally saw what Steph had noticed before. They were falling for each other, and they both deserved it.

"So, is that how you know your friend?" Justin asked.

I gazed into Justin's perfect hazel eyes. "What do you mean?"

"Well, they're clearly flirting. Are they together?" I guess I wasn't the only one who noticed.

"No, my brother is married to a woman." I watched my brother and best friend. If I didn't know them, I suppose I would have believed the same as Justin.

He seemed surprised. "Oh, I just assumed, sorry." Justin started to backpedal.

"No, it's fine. Seriously, don't worry about it." I wasn't about to tell Justin our entire family drama at this point, so keeping it to *Derrek and Steph are married* was easier. Besides, I didn't want to out my brother, he hadn't even told me. How would he feel if a complete stranger found out that he was into men?

"So, are you seeing anyone?" His question was shy, as if he was afraid to ask it.

I glanced in his direction, then immediately back at my brother and Ryan. "If I was, would I have brought my best friend on this cruise?" I smirked at the realization of just how pathetic a life I was truly living this week.

"Fair enough," he told me.

This was the perfect moment for him to fall in love with me. For him to give up his whole life and come be with me. At least that was the fantasy. If this were a romantic comedy or one of those contemporary romance novels, he would give it all up to be with me, but this was real life.

He pushed me into the water and said, "Let's join them."

I guess I was just going to be a friend. Which was clearly all I ever could be with him.

We joined their water fight and played like kids for about ten minutes, and I snapped a few pictures before we continued our trek up the waterfall.

We got to the steepest part of the climb, where it felt a little like rock climbing. I knew we were nearing the end and I was slightly disappointed. Justin said that he needed to get back to the ship immediately after we were done. I wanted more time. I had known Justin for only a few hours, but he was cute, seemed to be interested in me, and he was incredibly fun to be around. If we were back home, I wouldn't let him get away.

"So, are you going to be at the same bar you were at the other night?" I asked him through winded breath as I climbed over a large rock.

"Yeah, will I see you there tonight?" he asked.

"Maybe, we'll see if my family sends me into a downward spiral enough to show up already wasted." It was a joke, but there was a small part of me that figured it would happen again. My mother always knew how to get under my skin.

Justin laughed as he climbed another rock and assisted me up. "I think we lost your brother and friend." He looked around, trying to locate them.

"Oh shit, that's not good. I hope they're okay." I was going to be more pissed if they ditched us.

"So, and forgive me if this is inappropriate, but are they into each other?" he asked as we both waded in the water, still half looking for them.

I certainly hoped so, but I kept my mouth shut for the moment.

"Oh, there they are. They went the other way." Justin pointed them out as they climbed the side of the falls.

I was happy that they were safe, probably not good to lose my brother and fake fiancé on the same land adventure, probably wouldn't make for good dinner talk. However, there was a part of me that was a little disappointed, I was enjoying time alone with Justin.

Derrek and Ryan approached, drenched and laughing.

"This is the coolest thing I think I've ever done," Ryan exclaimed.

"You should try skydiving, mate," Justin offered as the group climbed another rock.

"That might be a bit much," Ryan scoffed.

Justin climbed one more rock and held my hand as I climbed with him. "Nah, you want to talk about a great experience? Free-falling from a plane—"

"A perfectly good plane, may I remind you," Ryan interrupted.

"But still, nothing feels freer," Justin finished.

He made it sound so cool, I almost wanted to do it. "Any chance you could sneak away a little longer and go skydiving with us?"

"Us?" Ryan seemed offended. "Baby girl, you are on your own here."

I laughed.

"Sorry, this is the only thing I have time for. But free drinks on me at the bar tonight. Just come and make me look cool for the boss," he pleaded.

"You got it." I provided a thumbs-up with a smile.

Justin turned to me and said, "Sans you already being plastered, if possible."

"We'll keep her under control." Derrek placed his hands on my shoulders and rested his cheek against mine.

"Good." Justin winked at me.

What did that wink mean? I hated when men gave me mixed signals. They either want to be with you, or they don't. Not that we could have a relationship, but at least we could fool around a little, and ease some tension. That's all I wanted, right?

"Better dress sexy," Ryan whispered to me.

I elbowed him in the gut. How dare he say that where Justin might hear.

We continued all the way up the falls and congregated as a group at the end of the trail back toward the shuttle.

"God, that was fun!" Ryan was still on a high from climbing the falls. "Is it bad that I want to go back down and do it again?"

"There are a thousand other things we can do around here," Derrek told him.

"Okay, so what do we do next?" Ryan asked.

"Well, I head back to the ship," Justin announced.

No, I wanted more time with him. I needed to see how set in stone this need to go back to the ship was. There was no get-to-know-each-other time when he would be tending bar. "Come on, there's gotta be time for one more thing." I egged him on, hoping for something from him.

Justin looked at his watch. "I guess we could do one more excursion."

"Skydiving!" I blurted out. I had always wanted to go skydiving, and I thought today was the perfect time to risk my life with a man I met two days ago.

"I don't know if I have time for that. That can take hours," he told me.

"Then, maybe just a stroll through town?" I asked.

Justin nodded. "That, I can do."

I was disappointed. I wanted to go skydiving. I was finally brave enough to get off my ass and do it. Maybe I was trying to impress Justin. How do you impress a guy that comes from the country with nothing but animals that want to kill you?

Justin took a deep breath as he looked at me. "If I'm late to my shift all because you wanted to go skydiving, you're not getting free drinks." He gave in.

I smiled and hopped up and down a little in excitement. "Yay."

"Yeah, you two do that, the shopping around town sounds much … safer," Ryan said as he gestured to Derrek to follow.

"Your loss, boys," Justin said as he wrapped his arm around me, and we made our way to call a taxi.

I turned to Derrek and Ryan and exclaimed, "Head to the beach. We're meeting the family in a couple of hours!"

"Got it, sis," Derrek's voice rang out.

"So, have you ever gone skydiving before?" Justin asked.

I shook my head. "Always wanted to, never did."

"Well, you're in for a treat," he told me.

We hailed a cab and Justin advised where we were going.

"So, what's the story?" he asked. "You show up at my bar, totally munted, and apparently, it's because of your crazy family. One of which can't possibly be your brother."

"Munted?" I asked.

"It means drunk, okay?" Justin rolled his eyes. "It's Australian."

I let out a slight chuckle. "Okay." I wasn't sure how much I wanted to unload to Justin this early in our not-going-anywhere-not-even-a-relationship relationship. But if this week ended with a hookup with a hot Australian, I was game. Then again, if I told him everything, he might abandon me right here right now. "My mother is very traditional," I started.

"And you're not."

I shook my head. "She's desperate for me to get married and have a ton of kids like my older sister."

"And you don't want that?" I wasn't sure if he was surprised or disappointed.

The older I got the harder it was to find a man that didn't want children as well. I was starting to get a sense that Justin was one of those guys that longed for children eventually. I didn't want kids, and so many people in my life would act like the world would stop turning at this singular decision. "I have nothing against marriage, but kids, that just seems like a lot," I explained. "I have three nieces and a nephew, and they exhaust me. I only get them in little spurts, and I am exhausted."

"That the only reason?"

I shook my head. "I also can't stand when babies are crying in public. I hate when I'm in a restaurant and there's a kid whining. It just totally ruins my whole night." I knew it sounded harsh, but it was true. "And don't feed me the it's-different-when-they-are-yours bullshit." That was always the next thing that came out of people's mouths.

"So, they exhaust and annoy you." He didn't seem to buy it.

"And I want to travel, without the stress of having kids around," I told him. I looked at him. "Do you want kids?"

"Oh, I couldn't want anything less. I'm on your side here." He sat back and reclined as much as he could in the taxi.

"Why don't you want kids?" I asked.

"Oh, the genes are not good. Depression, generational abuse, receding hairlines." He was half joking on the last one. "I just wasn't raised by the best parents. Who knows if I could even be a good dad, and the genes are going against the kid already." He shook his head. "Any kid I would have, would not make it far in life."

I was amazed at how honest he was about it. "I'm sorry." I could only imagine one or both of his parents abused him as a kid. I might resent my mother for being overbearing and my dad for being practically nonexistent, but I would take that over abuse any day.

He shrugged. "It's okay. They're back in Melbourne and I'm here." He moved closer. "With you."

Would it be weird to kiss him at this moment? Is that what he was hoping for? An invitation? Hell, if that's what he was wanting, I was willing to have sex with him in the back of this taxi.

The taxi came to a stop, and I looked out the window. Parachutes were falling from the sky. I suddenly felt nervous again. What was I doing? I was impulsively about to jump out of an airplane with someone I hardly knew.

"Ready?" he asked.

I didn't know how to answer that. Was I ready? No. Was I going to do this because I didn't want him to think I was a chicken? Yes. I nodded with a nervous smile.

Justin held out his hand for me and assisted me from the taxi. "Let's see how long the wait is. These are fourteen-passenger planes, so seven jumps at a time."

There was this part of me that had hoped the wait was like four hours. I would act all disappointed and then we would head back to town.

"We just had a cancellation and can squeeze you in on the next flight, if you'd like," the large Jamaican man behind the counter said to Justin.

"Awesome." He turned to me with a big smile.

If you have never gone skydiving, let me tell you, it is an intense start to any adventure. They hand you a pile of papers where you are basically signing your life away. Promising that if the worst were to happen, you, if you lived, or your family, if you didn't, wouldn't sue the place in which you went skydiving, the tandem instructor, nor the man who invented tandem skydiving. Then we watched an instructional video about how tandem skydiving works. I was now terrified. I dug my phone out of my bag, hoping there was Wi-Fi here so I could use it. Sure enough, there was. I looked up the percentage in which skydives fail. The statistics made me feel slightly better. Out of millions of skydives only like eleven to fifteen people die a year. *Here's hoping I'm not one of those fifteen.*

My least favorite part of the sign-in process wasn't even the signing my life away. It was when they made me step on a scale. Not that the number bothered me. I was a proud two-hundred-pound woman. It took a lot of years to be proud of it, but I was confident, and no one was going to shame me. I hated it because of the principle. I understood they needed to know to pair you with the right tandem instructor, but the fact that a bunch of people would publicly know my weight was bothersome, but I wanted to do this. I hopped on the scale and saw the slightly higher than two hundred number and hopped off.

We then had to take a class on how to skydive.

"So, when your tandem instructor taps your shoulder, you need to sprawl out like this." The instructor laid down on the ground on his stomach and held his arms and legs out and slightly elevated his head. "Got it?"

The group nodded.

We then walked to a plane, and he explained how and where to stand when it was time to tumble out at 13,000 feet. This was much larger than the one a friend of mine jumped out of once. She told me that she had to put her foot outside of the plane on a ledge right over the wheels. I was just glad I wasn't going to have to do that kind of jump.

Once the lesson was over, we got into our gear and the plane went up. The plane climbed over the island. I looked and saw the ship off in the distance. We popped up over the sparse number of clouds, and the plane finally stopped climbing.

My tandem instructor walked up to me; he could probably tell I was nervous. "You'll be fine." He gently touched my shoulder. His accent was thick but easily understood.

"How long have you been doing this?" I asked.

"First time." His face was serious, not a hint of sarcasm or levity.

My eyes widened in fear.

"Okay, not the best time to make that joke. I've been doing this for ten years. You're safe." He patted me on the shoulder with a slight chuckle at how gullible I was.

I smiled. "Yeah, let's not make jokes like that."

He strapped himself onto my harness and we approached the now-open door of the plane. A couple had already jumped. Now it was my turn.

"See you at the bottom," Justin yelled over the wind from the open door. He jokingly saluted me as he smiled and gave me a wink.

I nodded and gave him a thumbs-up.

We stood at the edge of the plane. I saw pretty much nothing but the ocean under us. I realized just how high up we were. The guy at the bottom said that we would be freefalling for ninety seconds, ninety seconds of falling from the sky. How are you in the air that long? I remembered them telling us that we would be climbing to about 13,000 feet. I did quick math in my head. "That's more than three miles in the air." And here I genuinely just assumed jets flew at a mile high because of the whole "mile-high club" concept. This put a lot of things into perspective for me.

I closed my eyes and waited for the fall to start. We tumbled out of the plane and began our freefall. After a few seconds, the tap came on my shoulder, and I sprawled out my arms and legs. I then opened my eyes and realized I was flying. I let out a scream like you do on the first drop of a roller coaster. It was a release of energy, of all the fear I had right before I opened my eyes, all the pent-up anger toward my mother. I wasn't scared. I was excited. I felt the adrenaline rush through my body, and I felt free. I was flying!

After ninety seconds, I felt a relatively violent pull as the parachute expelled and brought us to a quick decline in speed. My heart rushed as the adrenaline still coursed through my veins. "Oh my God, that was amazing!" I cried out. I had never felt so free in my life. No one could touch me up here.

My tandem instructor laughed as he handed me a couple of handles. "Here, would you like to steer?"

I grabbed them, confused. "You steer?"

"Well yeah, how else do you expect us to land at the landing zone?"

It made sense. I tugged on each handle to my side at the tandem instructor's command. The ground came closer and closer. I peered up, hoping to see Justin on his jump, but I saw nothing.

Once safely on the ground and disconnected from my tandem instructor, I looked back up at the sky. Another parachute was coming down. It was Justin. They too landed without any issues, and I ran up to him. "You were right!" I could still feel my heart racing.

"Exhilarating, isn't it?"

"It felt like I was flying!" I fell into his arms, and we hugged. As I reluctantly pulled away from him, our eyes met. Our noses were mere inches away from each other. My heart picked up speed. I wanted to kiss him. I could blame it on the high, the adrenaline rush from the skydive. He couldn't be too angry with me for that, right? I tried to talk myself out of it. I knew it would only complicate things more.

Turns out, I didn't have to. Suddenly, our lips met.

"Sorry," he said as he pulled away.

"It's okay." Talk about a rush.

CHAPTER 10

RYAN

Derrek and I started our stroll in downtown Ocho Rios, looking at all the colorful buildings and street merchants. I had never experienced anything like this before. It was incredible. Growing up, we didn't have the kind of money it would take to have a trip like this. I looked at Derrek, who seemed to be well-versed in travel.

"Your sister's crazy," I told him.

"You're only just realizing that?" Derrek shot back.

Lori had always been known to be on the adventurous side. Skydiving shouldn't have surprised me. She constantly talked about taking a trip to Niagara Falls and doing a zipline over the Canadian side of the falls. "Not even a little."

"Glad you're staying on the ground with me," Derrek said as he looked at a shop. "I should probably buy Stephanie a gift." He seemed sad.

"So, what happened?" I wanted to know what made him feel so unsatisfied with his wife. They always seemed like best friends.

Derrek shrugged. "I don't know. I just know that the life I have right now isn't the life I want." He turned to me. "But let's not talk about that. Let's just have fun."

I nodded in agreement. We walked around the shop looking for a gift for his soon-to-be ex-wife. I found a little trinket that looked like a mother holding a baby. I approached Derrek. "How about this?" I handed it to him.

He smiled. "I think it's perfect." He kept looking at it. "I'm excited to be a dad." I could hear a flutter in his voice, trying to hold in tears.

I placed my hand on his back. "I don't think anyone thinks otherwise."

"Steph does," he admitted, losing the battle with those tears fighting their way out.

I shook my head. "I'm sure she's just hurt. I'm sure she says things out of anger that she doesn't mean."

Derrek placed his fingers on his temples, trying to get him out of the mindset he was falling into, and looked at me. "I know." He walked up to the counter to pay for the gift.

We continued down the street. The buildings were colorful and the sound from street musicians made the atmosphere playful. We took in the salt air. It seemed to lighten Derrek's mood. I wanted to do more to help, but I worried even he didn't know why he was so unhappy.

"So, are you seeing anyone back in Los Angeles?" Derrek asked.

"No." I had a lot of dates and hooked up a few times, but I hadn't been in a real relationship in a couple of years. "Ricky destroyed any trust I have in men." I then laughed and said, "Sometimes it seems easier to be straight."

"Trust me, it's not." Derrek laughed.

"I wonder if your sister is plummeting toward the ground." I shuddered at the thought of it.

"I could never do that. I'm terrified of heights and more importantly, falling from them, so skydiving? Hell no." Derrek chuckled. He noticed a bakery. "Want a snack?"

I nodded. "Sounds great."

We entered the little bakery, which was filled with cakes, cupcakes, and cake pops. I had a major sweet tooth, and I wanted to eat no less than one each.

I approached the counter and pulled out my wallet. "On me," I wasn't going to take no for an answer.

"Sure, but then I'll get you a drink later," Derrek responded with the same urgency.

"Justin said free drinks."

"I'm sure there's a cut-off there." Derrek brought up a good point. The three of us together had the potential of sending that bar in the red from one night of free drinks. We weren't opposed to partying hard.

"Fair enough."

"I will take a chocolate one. Surprise me on what type I get." Derrek seemed overwhelmed by the options.

"I'll take lemon." I turned to Derrek. "We can split them."

Derrek smiled and nodded.

Once we received our orders, we sat on a patio table outside that overlooked the pier where the ship was docked.

"So, lunch is at Margaritaville; then we are going to the beach outside their property to swim and hang out." Derrek gave me the lowdown.

I split the two cupcakes in half and handed half of each to Derrek. "Sounds good."

"Hopefully, my sister is back from her death-defying adventure with that bartender soon." I could tell he was worried about her. Her adventurous existence always seemed to be a burden to Derrek. He was the younger brother, but he seemed to always be the one reining her in.

"How do you like Justin?" I wanted to know his take on his sister's newest attraction.

He shrugged as he took a bite of the chocolate cupcake. "If he's interested, they'll probably hookup on the ship, but then they will never see each other again. Who am I to have an opinion?"

Lori and I had the same pattern since our last breakups. She would find interest in a guy and hookup with him. However, once things seemed to get serious, she would break things off out of fear that he was going to cheat on her. She would always give a lame excuse about his height or his restaurant preferences. She would then basically ghost the poor guy and mope around saying how difficult it was to find a good man these days. This was easier since he lived on a cruise ship on the opposite ocean than where we lived. She wasn't much about having lasting relationships. Her last boyfriend was more than a year ago. Even then, she had trouble committing. He gave her a key to his place, and she promptly lost it. She never loses things, but that she lost. Derrek and I joked that it was because she didn't want to commit to Luke.

I was convinced her fear of commitment came directly from her terrible relationship with her mother. She resented her mother for resenting her, ergo, no long-term commitment just to spite her mother. It was clearer than ever this week. There was always this part of me that cheered her on, though, so I smiled and said, "What if Justin's the one?"

"What and she's going to give up her trajectory of taking over the animation studio you two work at to gallivant around on a cruise ship forever?" Derrek licked some of the frosting off his cupcake.

He brought up a good point. How would it ever work? He would have to move to LA, or she would have to give up her dreams. I guess the idea of those two being together was dead. However, the dream that I had had forever seemed closer and closer every moment I spent with Derrek.

We finished our cupcakes and decided to walk a little longer.

"There's gotta be something we can do aside from just walking around." I looked at everything around for something that seemed halfway interesting.

"We could get in a cab and do the swamp tour," he offered. "We did it when we were kids, and it was pretty cool, you can pet Crocs."

"You don't mean the shoes, do you?" I asked hesitantly.

"Hey, you wanted to do something."

Petting one of the most dangerous animals on this planet was not what I had in mind. I nodded. "Sounds like a fun late-morning trek."

We hailed a cab and got to the reserve. We were greeted by kind tour guides and paid for our excursion.

It started off easily as we walked through an area with birds flying around. It was fun, we were in the cage with the birds. I could reach out and touch a peacock if I wanted.

Tarone was our guide's name. He seemed young, barely out of university, and smiled a lot. "Here." He said as he handed me seeds from a bowl, "You can feed the birds." He offered.

I took them and started sprinkling them down on the ground.

Tarone grabbed my hand and guided me down to the peacock's beak. So, the bird could eat directly from my hand, "You can feed them like this."

"Thanks." It was cool to have a peacock eat out of my hand. I looked up at Derrek and we smiled back and forth. I decided to pretend we were on a date. I wanted so desperately for it to be real. Even though it was a weird idea for a date, it still would have felt so romantic.

After the seeds were gone, we continued the walk. Later, we entered an area full of reptiles, "Lori would be in heaven." I whispered to Derrek.

He chuckled.

We walked up to a tank with snakes in it. "Those look wild."

Tarone walked up to us again and asked, "Would you like to hold one?"

"They're not poisonous, right?" I asked, half kidding since I can't imagine they would hand random people dangerous snakes.

"You mean venomous? Of course not," Tarone advised.

I was confused. "What's the difference?"

"Venom is injected, and poison is ingested," he explained as he pulled out a large snake from the cage. "This one is very friendly." He handed it to me.

I took it and held it like I was just handed an ancient one-of-a-kind vase. I didn't know how to handle a snake that was probably looking at me like I was lunch.

"You okay there?" Derrek was standing there making fun of me.

"I'm good," I said, then under my breath thought out loud, "Starting to wish I had gone skydiving." I could feel the snake wrap around my arm, and it squeezed hard. I could feel my circulation get cut off. "So, that's why they call them constrictors," I said to him as I analyzed what was happening with the snake.

My friendly snake was put away and we continued down the path.

Tarone stopped at another cage, and I saw yet a bigger snake.

"What the hell?" Derrek asked in shock.

"That's an anaconda," Tarone said to us.

I had never seen one in person before. "That could eat a human, couldn't it."

"Yes, it's rare, but they are capable of eating humans," Tarone explained to us

"Let's move on." I pushed Derrek away from the cage and we continued moving down the path. In a smaller cage, I saw a massive lizard, "What is that?"

"An Iguana," Derrek answered. "You'll probably see a few in the wild on this trip."

The thought that a lizard that massive could just be walking around on its own was terrifying. "Is it dangerous?"

"The tail can be, yes. But they aren't aggressive if you leave them alone." Tarone answered.

"What does that thing eat?" I asked, expecting him to say small dogs, cats, or goats. I felt like I was staring down the T-Rex in Jurassic Park.

"They are strictly vegetarians." Was not the answer I was expecting from Tarone.

We were then led to some more cages until we reached a pit. I looked down, and there they were. Crocodiles. "Those are huge." I looked at the pile of crocodiles sunbathing.

"Yeah, aren't they cool?" Derrek asked as we gazed down at them.

As long as they couldn't eat me, I was perfectly fine. Those I know have and will eat humans if given the chance.

We spent the rest of the trip seeing all the animals and learning a little more about each one from Tarone. We saw Warthogs, different kinds of deer, and wombats, which made me think of Lori and

Justin again and wonder how they were making out, and if they were *actually* making out.

After the tour, I smiled at Derrek. This is what I wanted. It's what I had always dreamed of. No stress, no drama, just a nice time out with a guy I cared about. I wanted to tell him how I felt, but what if he *was* straight? I had always had my suspicions, and I always prided myself on *knowing*. But what if I was off just because I was attracted to him?

"This has been such a fun day. Thank you for getting my mind off of everything happening in my marriage." Derrek said to me.

"You're welcome. I'm still here if you want to talk," I offered.

"Thanks, but right now, may not be the time to do that." Derrek was being vague.

"Sure, whenever you're ready," I told him.

We hailed a cab and headed back to town to meet everyone for lunch and beach time. It was nice to pretend like Derrek was my boyfriend for the last couple of hours, but it was time to go back to basic friendship as to not blow my cover with Lori nor to cause any drama about Derrek and Steph's failing marriage. The last thing I wanted to do was to cause anymore drama in this already dramatic family.

CHAPTER 11

LORI

After Justin and I got back to town, we said our goodbyes as he rushed back to the ship, and I went to go meet my family for lunch at the Margaritaville right on the beach.

I saw Ryan, "Hey, there you are!" I called out.

"How was your skydiving adventure?" He asked.

"It was amazing." I wasn't about to slip out that we kissed. I couldn't wait to see Justin again later. I was hoping that after his shift we could sneak away and do more of that.

"As freeing as Justin said it would be?" He asked.

I nodded, "You have no idea."

Ryan laughed, "And I never will." He held out his arm for me to take his, "I've been waiting out here for you so we could arrive together."

He was such a great friend for helping me lie to my family. I took his arm, and we walked in together.

"There they are." My mother seemed already pretty liquored up. Maybe she would be relaxed enough to not cause trouble. She rose from her seat with a drink in hand and approached us. "You two are so sweet together." Forget pretty liquored up, my mother was drunk. She pulled us in for the most uncomfortable group hug I had ever been a part of.

Ryan and I sat down with the rest of the family.

Kasey put down her drink and asked, "So, what did you two do this morning?"

"We climbed Dunn's River, then Lori went skydiving and I went on a nature walk," Ryan explained.

"You two split up for part of the day?" Dave asked.

I looked at Ryan, how would we explain our separate days? The fact that I was on a possible date with a hot Australian bartender. I was still confused about the kiss.

"Well, Lori wanted to go skydiving, and Derrek and I didn't," Ryan explained.

"So, you two left her all alone?" Kasey asked.

"No…" Ryan's no trailed off as he clearly was trying to think of some sort of answer.

"We met a friend the other night and I went with her …" I looked at Ryan and Derrek. "Her name is Justine and she's from Australia. She happened to be alone on the way up the falls, so we invited her to hang out with us. She and I wanted to go skydiving and the boys didn't."

"Oh, well that's nice." My mother slurred her words.

"How many has she had?" I asked.

"A few," my father admitted.

I knew Mom would panic if she thought I spent any time alone with a boy. I was barely allowed to have guy friends growing up. My mom thought it was "inappropriate" for girls and boys to hang out one on one or some weird shit like that unless they planned on getting married or whatever. She couldn't believe that men and women could become friends. One of my best friends in high school came out as pansexual so I challenged that belief of my mom's when I asked if this meant she couldn't hang out with anyone, which of course my mother found ridiculous. I just figured it would be best to lie since Ryan already slipped up that we hadn't spent the day together.

We waited for our table to be ready, which took some time since we were such a huge party. We sat down and had our first truly pleasant meal as a family on this trip, which was very nice. The family that my parents tried so hard to make look perfect from the outside was

genuinely imploding. I was lying to my parents, Derrek and Steph were splitting up, and I was starting to worry that Kasey had a deep dark secret that no one knew about because she couldn't be *that* perfect.

After lunch, the adults sat with drinks in our hands laying in the sun while the kids splashed around in the ocean.

I just kept thinking about meeting up with Justin later. I watched the kids play and realized how simple it all was back then. When my mother wasn't hounding me about marriage and adding to our already overpopulated earth, when I didn't have to lie just to appease her, or when neither of us had to be drunk to be civil. When all that mattered was my sister not bugging me and my brother staying out of my room. I knew I was a disappointment to my mom and the only reason she acted crazy was because she wanted what she thought was best for me. I also knew that didn't excuse what she said to me, but at least I understood. The choice I needed to start making was this a relationship I wanted to continue, or was it too toxic for both of us?

Later, I heard the loud blast of the horn as we pulled out of port. Ryan came running to me. "What? We aren't gonna wave at random people?"

I laughed. "That's only for the start of the trip."

He shook his head. "I will never understand this life."

"How was your day with my brother?" I was hoping that maybe the two connected.

He nodded, "We had a great time." He glanced down at his feet, "I just wish I had more clarity about my feelings and his feelings." It was nice that at least one of them admitted to me that he liked the other.

I knew in my heart that Ryan always had feelings for Derrek. It was hard to see the two of them together when I thought that

Derrek was happy in his marriage to Steph. Now that I knew he wasn't and wanted out so he could explore this other side of himself that was attracted to men, I just wanted them both to be happy. "Why don't you just ask him on an actual date?

"He's still married to a woman." He reminded me.

"But he's getting a divorce," I told him. "You never know what might happen if you just ask."

"Says the girl that has always gotten a yes out of any guy that she's asked out," Ryan blurted out.

"That's not fair." I argued, "It took a long time for me to even get the courage and pretend I loved myself for me to *actually* start loving myself." Growing up in a larger body was always difficult. I was made fun of a lot for it, and doctors didn't take my health seriously because I am constantly met with "just lose weight." I was always lucky that at least my immediate family has always accepted my size. It took *me* accepting my body for what it is and loving it fully before I started to believe I was worthy of the men I was attracted to. Once I had that confidence knowing I was worthy, it was easy for men to find *that* attractive.

"You think that your brother, who has been married to a woman and has never shown any interest in men or me, would be okay with me asking him out?" Ryan was clearly not believing it was even possible. "This will just stay what it is, a fantasy. Which you would know nothing about."

I didn't think that was fair, "I have had so many fantasies with celebrities." I countered.

He laughed, "That's not the same," he looked around, "You *know* you're not gonna get with a celebrity. It's an easy unrequited love. When you *know* the person, it becomes this weird need." He explained.

I didn't understand what he meant, "But it's still a fantasy."

"But a fantasy that your mind makes you think is real, and every time you're with that person, it becomes stronger. You imagine what it would be like to push that person against the wall and kiss them."

"Ew, that's my brother."

"And they like it." He sounded like that voice you hear in your head when you read romance novels. It was weird.

"With a celebrity, it's like, your brain knows it won't work. It's safe to have that fantasy and not get hurt when they have a new boyfriend or get married." His expression turned dark; he was sad.

I think that was when I finally got it. Not getting with that hot rookie LA Ram would never be as painful as him not getting with my brother. "I get it. I get it as much as I can."

Ryan nodded. "It's real and sucks." Tears were forming in his eyes as he proclaimed his pain.

I knew I couldn't help him, as much as I wanted to. Heartbreak can be eased my friends, but never healed. So, I just hugged him. "Wanna get a drink?" I asked through our hug.

"No, I just wanna be alone, kinda like you yesterday morning," he told me. He pulled away. "But you go and have fun with Justin." He winked at me.

I shook my head with a chuckle. "I'm engaged, remember?" I gave him a friendly punch in the chest and headed out to go drink, "I promise I'll come home *mostly* sober." I liked drinking, and I liked the feeling of being drunk. Plus, I was on vacation, so why not?

"Have fun."

I headed to the same bar we went to that first night. I figured it was safe to hit on him all night without getting caught. My sister and her husband had four kids, so no way they would come to the bar. My parents are in bed, generally, by nine, so chances of running into them while I was hitting on someone other than my best friend, slim. My brother and Steph already know the whole story, so I figured I was safe.

I stepped into the bar, and there he was, Justin. At the bar, slinging drinks like a pro. I wanted him to sling more than just drinks to me. Okay, that was bad, I wouldn't sound that bad when I was talking to him.

I plopped down on a barstool and smiled.

"Hey, where's your better half?" That Australian accent had me ready to hop into bed with him right at that moment. I don't know what it is about the Australian accent that gets to me, it's the only accent I like, and it gets me going.

"He is in our stateroom, and very very gay." I ran my hand through my brown straight hair and let my hand brush against my cleavage. I wanted him to know that I was very very available.

He smiled. "What can I get ya?"

I thought for a moment. "Cosmopolitan." It was my favorite drink, and it was invented in Minnesota and made famous by Sex and the City. Okay, so the invention is contested, but I'm a Minnesotan by birth so, I stand by it. It was a sexy drink, and everyone knew it.

"You got it."

It was weird. It seemed like a very bartender-and-customer kind of relationship. I glanced at my cowl-neck top and back at him. "You got a girlfriend?" It was a fair question; it shouldn't be too forward. Plus, he'd kissed me earlier that day.

He poured the Triple Sec into the mixer. "You don't date much when you work on these ships."

No girlfriend. I was going to bed this boy by the end of the week. "Are you here all night?"

He nodded. "Then I am headed back to my room in the crew space."

"Crew space?"

"There's a smaller section of the ship that is meant for the wait staff and other lower members of the ship that don't get to mingle with ship patrons off the clock." He finished pouring the cranberry juice, placed the top on the mixer and shook it vigorously. "It's like we're on a smaller cruise ship. We have a pool, staterooms, the works, just less luxurious. It's more like living in a sardine can, but I love my ship life."

I remembered seeing a pool I couldn't get to when I was a kid. "Is your pool at the very front of the ship?"

He nodded. "That's the staff pool." He handed me my drink.

"I remember seeing it before, I was pissed I couldn't go swimming in it. It looked a lot less busy."

Justin laughed. "Yeah, everyone is usually too busy to use it."

"Sounds like a shitty life." I took a sip of my Cosmo. There was always the possibility of getting him to see that there could be a better life outside of living on the ocean and we could have more than just a fling.

"Nah, I love my job. My uncle is high up in the company, I have a bit more freedom than other staff members. I still don't get to hang out off the clock, but I get a bit more freedom than other people I work with." He left to go help some other patrons and I nursed my cosmopolitan.

A guy approached me, "Hey pretty lady." He brushed his hand through his blonde hair and looked at me with his deep blue eyes. He was the perfect example of that jock that peaked in high school.

"Hi." But I wasn't against having a little fun, since bartender boy wasn't reciprocating my flirting. I didn't intend on having sex with this new guy, but a little friendly flirting never hurt anyone. Besides, if Justin was into me like he showed after our jump, it might make him jealous, and I wasn't against playing some games. I moved my hair, which was behind my ear to drape over my face.

"How are you alone on this ship?" he asked me.

Justin came back. "She's with her fiancé."

There it was, the jealousy that I was hoping to get out of him. I wasn't going to play nice though. I glared at him with a what-the-hell expression.

The blonde guy became nervous. "I'm so sorry." And he left.

"What the hell, Aussie?" I wanted him to admit that he wanted me.

"Is that my new nickname?" He smiled.

"Don't get cute, why did you do that?" I played more into my anger.

Justin looked at the guy who was now hitting on some other girl, "He's an asshole. He drags a drunk girl back to his stateroom every night."

"This is only the third night." I reminded him.

"He works here." Justin kept his gaze on the blond guy. "He's a Guest Experience staff member. His actual job description is to make guests feel at home, he *thinks* it's sleeping with any pretty girl that walks," he informed me.

"You guys can sleep with guests?" I asked, selfishly I might add.

Justin shook his head. "No, you can't. He'll get caught one day because a girl will call him on his shit."

I was a little disappointed. "I wasn't going to sleep with him. I just wanted to flirt a little. It's a nice ego boost to flirt."

"You need an ego boost?" His disbelief was annoying.

I shrugged, "My last relationship didn't end great, and all the shit with my mom." I unloaded, "Sometimes, I just need to feel sexy again." I loved myself and I knew I was pretty. Sometimes, I still struggle with society's disdain for fat girls, and mindless flirting helps get me back out of it.

Justin motioned toward him. "That your type?"

I turned my head back to look as well. "Not even a little."

"What is your type?"

I nervously met his gaze "I don't wanna say." It would be weird to tell the guy who was your type that he was your type.

"Come on. Is it the guy you're here with?"

"Gay? No."

"I mean the way he looks."

I shrugged. "Closer." I slid my now-empty glass back to Justin and smiled. "You're more my type."

Somehow, I had the courage to say it. "I have a three-hour break in about an hour. Wanna hang out, then go break some rules?" I wasn't sure exactly what he meant by that, but I was game.

"Hell yeah."

That hour passed very quickly when Justin put his apron off to the side of the bar as he walked around the other side and over to me, "Let's go break those rules." He held out his hand inviting me to take it.

"You got it." I let him pull me away.

He moved my arm to wrap around his, and he guided me through the ship.

"So, what rule were you planning on breaking?" I was hoping it was the hookup that I longed for. After the last few days on this ship, I would give anything for another release of energy, in the form of an orgasm this time.

"Well, you said you always wanted to swim in that pool you saw when you were younger." He stopped and got in my face, "Now's your chance." He winked.

Something inside of me got excited. I loved doing things that were against the rules, not illegal, but naughty.

My aunt got married when I was around nine years old, on a riverboat. She and her fiancé had only rented the upper level, so we weren't allowed downstairs. It was forbidden, so I needed to get down there. My cousin and I kept trying to sneak down the stairs, but we had responsible parents who watched us. So, I concocted this great idea that I would throw my shoe over the edge, then I had to go get it. So, that's what I did. My mother had a field day yelling at me about how dumb that was. She told me that it was beyond stupid and that I could have lost my favorite shoe forever off the edge of the boat. I was allowed to go and get my shoe, but my cousin couldn't come with me. So, I have always loved a chance to do something a little naughty, especially if it's forbidden.

"So, you like working on a cruise ship?" I wanted to get to know him better. I know this would if anything, end in a hookup. But he was a nice guy and I wanted to get to know him.

He nodded, "Yeah, it's a great life. I get to see so many incredible places and it's like I live on vacation."

"Do you live on the ship?" I couldn't imagine not having any time off the ship.

He shook his head, "I usually work eight months at a time." He explained.

"Eight months?" That sounded like a long time to be out to sea.

"Yeah, it's pretty normal. Our time on the ship varies, between four to ten months. I start in March and go until November. I get to spend Christmas with my family then go back to the ocean in March."

"Kinda sounds like my job."

"How so?"

"I work in television. So, we go on hiatus, plus you never know if your show is even gonna come back. So, I do get months off at a time whenever we aren't in production." It wasn't the same, I had a place I could call home, but he didn't.

"LA girl, huh?" he seemed to be mocking me.

"Originally from Minnesota, but I got the hell out of there as soon as high school was over." I loved Minnesota, it's a great place to visit, but I would never want to live there again.

"Isn't it always cold there?" A common misconception from anyone outside of the Midwest.

"It's cold for a good portion of the year, but we have extreme temps." I loved teaching people about Minnesota. People always pictured us sitting in igloos and thinking forty degrees was swimming weather.

"I wouldn't have guessed that."

"Yeah, we get super-hot and humid summers, and super dry cold winters," I explained.

"How cold does it get there?"

I shrugged. "I'm a dumb American, so I have no idea what it is in Celsius, but it can get as cold as fifty below zero, and I'm pretty sure your zero is our thirty-two." I knew a little about the metric system, but not much.

"Ooo, that's cold." He shuddered like he was expected to experience that kind of weather.

"So, how cold does it get where you live?"

He shook his head, "Not that cold, that's for sure."

"You said you were from Melbourne, right?"

He chuckled, "You do remember some of the night we met."

"Embarrassingly, yes." I hated being reminded of that night. I wanted to forget everything about it, especially when it came to my drunk ass around Justin. "But you also mentioned it earlier to me, that your parents are still there."

"Right." He pulled me to a door that said staff only, "This is the magic door."

"Magic door?" It sounded corny.

"This is the door that leads you into our portion of the ship." He was talking about the staff and crew members. "As a crew member,

I sleep in a sardine can that I have to share with another crew member. I'm one of the lowest members of the staff as a bartender." He opened the door and motioned his hand to allow me to enter.

"Ooo, the magic door." I mocked his term playfully.

He shook his head. "Shut up." He pushed me through the door.

We entered a long hallway with a lift at the other end, "This is how horror movies start." It did look quite questionable as we made our way down the corridor.

"I promise, you won't get murdered down here." We reached the lift and he put a key where the button should be. "Just pretend like you belong. No one should question that you're not a crew member."

I was hoping he was right; I didn't want him to get in trouble.

Justin guided me down a long white corridor with doors on either side. It seemed very clinical. There were large objects being tied back to the wall. We walked through a doorway with a hazard tape looking border around it, "What's that mean?" I asked.

"It's a watertight door, in case of flooding. It will help stabilize the ship."

"I guess you have to think about those things, don't you?" I realized how little I thought about the ship sinking because the crew had to handle it on their own.

He nodded as he led me down a couple flights of stairs. "Sorry, we don't get elevators." He told me.

I was confused, "I thought all the non-American English speakers call those lifts."

Justin let out a little laugh. "Aussie's, like me, like to switch it up. We call it both."

It was fun to spend some time with him. Though, I still wasn't convinced he wasn't going to murder me and throw me overboard.

We reached another door. He opened it and revealed what looked to be a cafeteria.

"This is the mess hall."

"So, you eat here?" I asked, trying to hide my dismay.

"Hey now, it's not bad." Justin looked over the high school cafeteria and dive diner lovechild of an eatery.

I bumped my shoulder into his. "Oh, come on. I just mean, with all the great food up there and you get what looks like college cafeteria food?" I saw a lot of other crew members around "Are you sure you won't get in trouble for bringing me down here?" I was willing to turn around and go back up if it meant saving him trouble.

"Nah, these crews are so big, no one ever knows who's who. I meet new people every day down here." I guess it shouldn't have surprised me, there had to be a lot of manpower to make these towns on water run. He shrugged, "Just keep acting like you belong."

"What should my story be?" I figured that I should have a story in case someone asked me what I did on the ship.

"No, stories get too complicated, you may run into someone in the same department." He had a point; it would be easier to get caught.

"So, what if someone asks me what department I work in?"

"You won't be alone, I'm with you."

"So, you're never gonna have to pee?" I knew that I would end up being alone at some point.

He turned me to face him, "You worry too much, no one is gonna ask you which department you work in."

I nodded. "okay. What first?"

"There's a party just down the hall." He pointed toward the left. "Wanna hit it?"

I nodded. "What's the party like?"

"Well, it's in the crew bar, so it's like any other party in a bar or club." As he led me closer to this place, I could hear loud beat-heavy music.

"What, like a rave?" I asked sarcastically.

"Not *as* crazy as your normal rave, but it is, as Americans would say, popping."

"Never say that." I let out a chuckle at his assumption of American slang.

Justin guided me into the party and there were hundreds of people inside this large normal looking bar. "So, who serves the drinks?" I pointed to the empty bar and yelled in Justin's direction.

"You ask a bartender." He pointed to himself.

"So, it's self-serve?" We walked toward the bar.

"Sometimes, sometimes someone will man it for the night, but we don't have a crew, so we just kinda take care of ourselves down here." He stepped behind the bar and made me another cosmopolitan and poured himself a gin and tonic. "Wanna dance?" he handed me the drink.

I nodded and walked with him out to the dance floor. We danced for about an hour when I finally got tired. I fanned myself, "Can we cool off?" I could barely hear anything but the music and the screaming people, I wasn't sure if he could even hear me.

Justin nodded and guided me out of the club, "Wanna hit that pool now?"

I heard a ringing in my ear. "Yeah, sounds good. Whatever stops permanent damage to my eardrums," I joked.

Justin guided me through a few more corridors, we passed a lot of people, some didn't give me a passing look. There were some that seemed to know I didn't belong, or maybe I was just being paranoid.

"One more door." He opened the last door, which revealed the dark starry night outside.

I stepped outside and peered up at the stars, "They are so beautiful." I glanced at Justin, "You don't get to see the stars much in Los Angeles."

"Same with Melbourne, too many city lights."

"LA has the lights, and the pollution." Los Angeles was always looked at as this dream city, but it was mostly gross, very polluted, and almost always on fire.

"I've heard LA is pretty smoggy." Justin took his shoes off and began soaking them in the pool.

I noticed that we were alone, "Why is no one here?" I was too busy looking at the stars to realize that the pool was empty.

"No one ever likes swimming at night. It's too cold for people who spend most of the year in the Caribbean." I guess it made sense, though, to someone who was born and raised in Minnesota, there was no way it could ever feel cold in the tropics.

"I will admit, I don't have the same stamina for the cold as I did before I lived in California." I came home for Christmas one year, and it was a warm Christmas, in the thirties. I could barely breathe outside because it was so cold. When I lived in Minnesota, I could handle zero like a champ.

"I'm sure Melbourne would feel cold if I ever went home for winter."

I slid out of my shoes and plopped down next to Justin, "I thought you said you went home for Christmas."

He put his hand in the water and splashed a little in my direction, "Americans, don't know much about the world, do they?"

I wasn't sure if I should be insulted, "Why?" I splashed him back.

"Because Christmas is during the summer in Australia." That was something I didn't realize.

"Wait, what?" It just didn't make sense to me.

"We have opposite seasons than America." He explained, "Our winter is June, July, and August."

"For real?" I pouted a little, "I guess Minnesota public education didn't do enough worldwide education. Then again, I was raised in a time when we thought Christopher Columbus was a hero."

"We never learned about him, other than that he discovered America." He told me.

"Don't say that in Minnesota, the Scandinavians will have your head, the Vikings were the true discoverers." I thought for a moment, "Then again, the natives were here long before anyone else."

"Well, my country was once just a very large prison." Another thing I didn't know about Australia.

"That explains a lot," I joked.

Justin shook his head with a chuckle, "I think you should go for a swim." He put his hand behind my head and pushed me right into the pool. He was lucky that I wasn't wearing something that was dry clean only.

I popped up from under the water and took a deep breath. I coughed a couple of times, "You asshole!" I went back under the water and found his ankles. I pulled him under with me.

We both broke the surface again, "I could have hit my head!"

"Well, you didn't." I splashed him with water.

Next thing we knew we were lost in a water fight in the pool, laughs and name calling. Once it was over, I swam up to him.

He pulled me closer. I felt his hands around my hips. He leaned in and kissed me again. This time the kiss was longer and stronger. It wasn't a quick peck. This meant something. I wrapped my legs around his waist, and he leaned against the wall of the pool.

I could taste the salt water on his tongue as it slid into my mouth. His hands caressed my back then explored down to my hips and butt again. I felt him hard, only our clothes between us. He pushed me against the wall of the pool as his kiss deepened. I wanted him, I needed him, and it seemed, he wanted me too. I was in heaven, and I didn't want to leave.

CHAPTER 12

RYAN

I was enjoying my night alone in the stateroom. I got a little reading done, watched a little TV, I even took a bit of a nap. I sat out looking at the stars, wondering how Lori was doing when I heard a knock on the door.

I moved toward the door and opened it. It was Lori's mom, tears in her eyes. The first thought that popped into my head was they had gotten into another fight. "Are you okay?" I asked.

"We have a problem." She sounded angrier than she did sad.

"What's going on?" I invited her into the stateroom. Now I was thinking that she found out that Derrek and Steph were getting divorced.

"Have you been in your room all night?"

"Yes," I answered nervously.

She wiped a tear from her eye and placed her now dampened hand on mine. "You are too good for my daughter. She is convinced that she will never settle down."

"Did you two have a fight tonight?" I asked.

She shook her head, "No, Jack and I were taking a night walk on the deck, and we saw her walking arm and arm with another man."

She must have meant Justin, I tried not to smile. I didn't want to show my excitement for my fake fiancé. According to her mom, she was cheating.

"She makes friends easily, you know that." This was a very true observation of Lori. She made friends everywhere she goes.

"That she walks arm and arm with? Sneaks into staff-only janitor's closets with?" She had a point.

"That doesn't sound like Lori, you sure it was her?" A janitor's closet doesn't seem like a place she would choose for a hookup.

"I know what my daughter looks like." She was not going to be convinced. We were caught.

"You sure it was a janitor's closet?" I needed to convince her that everything was alright, or I could distract her with another disaster in the family. I could just tell her about Derrek and Steph. No, that wasn't my story to tell.

"It said staff only." She told me.

"Okay, that Justine, she told you about earlier. It was, in truth, a man named Justin. I wasn't feeling well tonight, so she went out on her own." This didn't seem to calm her. I had to think fast, then it hit me. "Oh, shit. He was gonna take us to a staff-only party tonight." I lied, though I would later learn I accidentally told the truth.

"So, maybe it wasn't a janitor's closet." She seemed convinced, which was good.

"Trust me, if there's one thing your daughter isn't, it's a cheater." I paused for a moment. "She's been cheated on, she knows how it feels, and she would never cheat."

"She was cheated on?" Her mother was surprised. I guess I accidentally outed someone with a story that wasn't mine.

"Sorry, she never told you, I guess." I didn't know what to do, Lori would kill me if she found out I spilled a story like that to her mother. "Don't tell her I told you."

"I won't, I just wish she had told me herself." Her mom just seemed so disappointed. She plopped down on the bed.

I moved next to her and placed my arm around her shoulders and pressed my head against hers. "You can still fix this."

Her mom started crying. "How?" She seemed so hopeless.

To be honest, I had no idea how she could fix things with Lori. Lori was bullheaded and ready to write her mom off. I didn't know how to answer and knew I had to. "Honestly, I think the only thing to do is just be kind to her."

"I am nice to her." She never got it, that was clear.

"In your head, you were nice to her." I knew that this could either be a great revelation or it could be a complete disaster. "To her, you are passive-aggressive and controlling."

She broke from my grip and turned to me. "How dare you?" I guess this was a disaster. "You do not have children; you do not understand what it's like to watch your child make nothing but mistakes."

"That is *exactly* what I'm talking about." I stood to meet her glance, "She has made all kinds of great choices." Then it occurred to me, "So, she makes nothing but mistakes, what about me? You said I was too good for your own daughter. Clearly I'm not a mistake."

"You know what I mean."

"No, I don't." My anger built. The anger I had bottled up inside of me to try to keep the peace this week. She needed to back off her daughter. "She moved to a place to help her career, she has already won one massive award, and more are coming. She lives in a nice condo in a good city in the Los Angeles area, and she has been living with me for the last year, and you had no idea until four months ago!" I couldn't even look at her, "She has made all kinds of great choices."

She said nothing and walked out the door. The door slammed shut, and I finally felt like I could take a deep breath. "What a bitch." I thought things were better between the two of them, but it wasn't. I wanted Lori to get back, so I could talk to her, but she was busy getting laid by her Australian bartender. We got sloppy, and we failed at this masquerade.

I decided it was worth at least going out to look for her. When I opened the door Derrek was in my way, "Hey."

"Steph doesn't want me in our room." He was crying. "I don't know what to do."

I guess finding Lori was going to have to wait, "Come in."

We sat down on the bed, "I told her that I was into you." Why would he do that? He hadn't even told me how he felt. I have to be honest, my heart started fluttering at this revelation.

Derrek turned to me, "I want to come out to California and give it a try." He leaned in to kiss me.

I jerked back. I never thought I would do that if Derrek ever admitted that he wanted to be with me, but there was one glaring issue with his desire, "I don't want to be with someone who would abandon their kid."

"That's why I told her." He sulked into the room and sat on the corner of the king-size bed. "I wanted to see if she was willing to come out to California." He rose to his feet and meandered to the sliding glass door, "Pro-tip, not the thing to ask of someone who you are planning to divorce. She kicked me out."

I followed him through the sliding glass door onto the balcony that overlooked the wide-open ocean. This is what I had dreamt about since meeting Derrek. Somehow, it also scared me. I was going to be in the middle of a divorce, Derrek had no idea what it was he wanted yet, plus this meant long distance most likely. I just wished it wasn't so complicated.

"Any chance you could spend your off time in Minnesota, with me?" There it was the painful truth about someone who would be tied to Minnesota forever.

"Long-distance doesn't work, at least for me." I tried it with my first boyfriend. He moved away to college in New York. He had a dream of being on Broadway. He became very successful getting a smaller role in *The Lion King*, last I heard, he was an understudy for Hamilton. He broke my heart when his eye wandered to another actor, I just didn't share that passion, and he wanted someone who did.

"I get it."

"Derrek, I have honestly wanted this for a long time," I admitted. "But it just can't happen, not unless you and your family move to California." I was not willing to compromise on my career. I couldn't be an animator in Minnesota.

"With the way the world is now? You can freelance and set up an online business with rates. You can make a career that doesn't involve being on TV and Movies." It was clear he was desperate to compromise, was it bad that I wasn't willing to compromise on my dream? I had always dreamed of taking my mom to the movies and showing her the work I had done on it. It wouldn't be as impressive if I showed her a YouTube video.

"But this is my dream, and the money I would make from doing that is nothing compared to what I make out in California." I too was desperate. Desperate for him to understand that I couldn't just drop everything and move halfway across the country for a possible relationship. The fantasy was better than the reality, just as I had feared.

"The cost of living in Minnesota is lower, you don't need to make as much money." He looked out onto the ocean, his face filled with doubt and heartbreak. I couldn't handle seeing him hurt so bad.

Something came over me. I wasn't going to be the second person to break his heart tonight. I grabbed his shoulders, looked into his eyes, and I kissed him. I pushed him against the sliding glass door. At this moment, we were together, and that's all that mattered.

He wrapped his hands around my waist and pressed his tongue against my lips. I parted my lips and felt his tongue thrust into my mouth. Our tongues danced together. Maybe the fantasy and the reality could be good. I just needed to live in this moment forever.

I moaned as we kissed, I wasn't sure how far he wanted to go, and I wasn't opposed to having him, but he had never, to my knowledge, had sex with a man before. I reached around and touched his taut butt.

He removed his hands from my waist and pulled away to take his shirt off. He revealed his very fit upper body. His abs were so perfectly textured as if he was an airbrushed model on a magazine cover.

"You sure you don't wanna come out to California and model?" My words were taxed as I could barely breathe. He smirked at my words. I felt myself harden as I looked at him. *If this turns out to be a fucking dream I will be so pissed.* I thought to myself as I slid my shirt off. I took his hand and guided him back into the stateroom. I collapsed back into him.

His hands explored my chest and abs which only made my dick harder and longing for him more. This wasn't a hookup, this felt nothing like a hookup. Hookups, for me, are quick and meaningless. We both knew that this was deep and meaningful. This was how relationship sex feels when the relationship is good. It had been a long time since my last relationship, and I was aching for that feeling again. Especially since I was finally living out my fantasy that I had been living in for far longer than I cared to ever admit, and probably the reason why my relationships with men never worked, after I met Derrek.

I felt his hand creeping down my pants, one reason to not wear skinny jeans. I pulled away, turned him, and pushed him down onto the bed. "Do you want this?" I wanted to make sure I had full consent, especially since this was his first time with a man.

"Yes." He didn't even blink.

"Okay." I grabbed my shirt and slid it over my head covering my now sweaty chest.

"Wait, what are you doing?" I guess I didn't think about how weird it looked.

"Since I was sharing a bed with your sister, I didn't anticipate sex." I hurried to the door, "I need condoms, and God willing, lube."

"Umm, you can't get me pregnant." Derrek sat on the bed, looking at me.

"Doesn't change the fact that I've had a few hookups. While I have always been safe about them, you never know. I can get tested when we get back to the mainland." I was about ninety-nine percent sure that I hadn't picked anything up, but you never know and that would definitely be a mood killer, but so was leaving a hot horny man in my room while I decided to be responsible about the last few months.

I didn't want his libido to die, I didn't want my practicality to ruin the moment. I hurried to the lift and hit the button for the plaza level over and over hoping it would make the lift move faster. I let go and bounced up and down as I waited for the slowest elevator in the world to move down three levels. It felt like that elevator ride lasted an hour. The door finally opened, and I rushed toward the convenience store, praying it was still open.

The shop was open, and I nearly cried out, "Thank God" as I ran into the store.

I burst in, "Sorry, real quick, condoms and lube." No time to be subtle, especially when I was hard and trying to hide it.

The guy chuckled to himself a little and reached behind the counter. He handed me a couple of boxes of condoms, "Not enough planning before hitting the ship? Take your pick."

I grabbed the box I wanted. "You could say that." I looked around. "Lube?" hoping this place had some.

"Sorry."

Well, that was unfortunate, not a deal breaker, but sucky. I looked around and found a bunch of aloe vera. "We have a winner," I whispered to myself as I searched the ingredients. I found one that was pure. I handed it to the guy. "If you didn't know, this works great."

He took it from me. "Grab me a bottle?" He blushed.

I winked as I handed him a second bottle. "Action happens on the ship, huh?"

"You have no idea."

"Cool." He rung me up and I handed him my card. I turned back to him as I was leaving. "Thanks, man."

I dashed back to the lift.

I reached the stateroom again and found Derrek, asleep on the bed. "Damn." I threw the bag of Aloe and condoms into the corner. I lowered myself down into the bed, and I just stared at him for the next couple of hours.

I heard the door open, it was Lori, "Oh God. Ew."

I sat up. "No, he fell asleep. Nothing happened." I looked at him then glanced back at her, "So, how were things with the hot bartender?"

"We kissed."

"And…"

"We were in the staff only pool, and it was hot." She sat at the foot of the bed.

"So, nothing more than that?"

"I think we both chickened out." She seemed disappointed.

"Sorry."

"So, I don't get a bed tonight, huh?" She looked out at the balcony. "Maybe I'll just sleep under the stars."

"Steph kicked him out," I admitted to her. "I don't know what to do."

"And I suppose me showing up in her room wouldn't work because she'd probably guess where he was."

I laughed. "Right."

"So, under the stars, it is." She walked to the closet by the door and pulled out some blankets. "This may be enough to keep me somewhat comfortable."

"Why don't they have a couch or something?" I couldn't believe that all that was in here was a bed, a dresser, and a TV.

"Some rooms do, others don't. It all depends." She explained to me, "It was just the two of us, so we just needed a single berth."

I rolled my eyes, "Think the bed is big enough for all three of us? He's pretty broken up; he probably needs his sister."

She nodded, "It is a King." She curled up next to her brother and kissed him on the head. "I love you, baby brother." She whispered.

I smiled and laid back down and put my hand on his, "It's gonna be okay."

Lori and I fell asleep with her brother between us.

The next morning, I woke up to immediate eye contact with Derrek, "Morning." I whispered.

"Morning," He responded. "Sorry for falling asleep last night."

"You have nothing to apologize for, you have a lot going on, it was probably for the best." I wanted him to understand that I was not angry with him. I glanced past him, "Your sister is up before anyone else, as always."

"She was up before me; I haven't seen her." Derrek sat up and peered outside on the balcony.

She was out there, leaning against the railing staring off into the distance.

"Every cruise we've been on, she's spent most of her time out there. Every time we ask her why, she always just says 'thinking.' Sometimes I worry she has some mental health stuff going on that she just doesn't talk about."

I had worried about that myself, she always needed to think and sometimes wanted to just be left alone, and when you're an extrovert, it's unusual. "She's got a lot going on." I tried hard to not tell him how I felt about their mother, but I just couldn't keep it in, "Your mother's a real bitch."

Derrek was quiet.

"I don't mean to offend you; she came over last night—" I was cut off.

"No, you're right." He kept looking at his sister, "It's one of the reasons I felt like I couldn't come out. My parents would be fine with me being gay, or whatever I am, but it just didn't fit into Mom's idea of my future."

"Isn't that the same thing as having issues with you being bi?" I assumed that was how he would eventually identify.

"First of all, I don't know what I am, yet, and second, it's not like they would be angry with me for liking men. She would just be disappointed that I wouldn't give her biological children."

"What is your mother's obsession with children? And besides gay couples can get a surrogate and have biological children."

"Mom comes from a generation where things like that didn't exist, and people got married to have children." He fell back down into the bed, "Sometimes I wonder if she ever loved Dad or she just got married."

"You think your parents don't love each other?"

"I mean think about it, what if mom was just spoon-fed the same things she told us, and she felt like she had to get married to be complete." He sat back up with a realization on his face. "What if she's a lesbian?"

"What?"

He looked at me. "Seriously, what if she's into women but did what I did." His realization turned into desperation. "What if she has always been miserable but trying to make her parents proud of her,"

"Like you?"

"Like me."

I placed my hand on his back. "But you're fixing it."

"But, if she's like me, I want her to fix it too."

"Who's like you?" Lori asked as she shut the sliding glass door behind her.

"He's worried that your mom is like him and miserable in her marriage," I informed her.

She came to the bed and grabbed his hand, "If she is, that's something she needs to come to terms with. It's not your demon to bear." She kissed his hand and pulled him in for a hug. "You have enough to worry about in your life."

"By the way, your mom was here last night, she saw you with that Aussie." I finally told Lori.

"Wait, when?" Lori's voice was urgent and full of panic.

"I guess your parents were taking a nightly stroll down the promenade when they saw you walking arm and arm with him."

"That's how you knew something happened with him." Her panic calmed into more of a worry.

"It's fine, I covered. I said that we had both made plans with him, but I wasn't feeling well, so I stayed behind." I looked at her judgingly, "As long as you were on your best behavior, everything should be fine."

"Which, I was." She contested.

"So, you went out for drinks with him last night?" Derrek asked her. "Do you think this would be more than a hookup?"

"It would end up being long distance, and like forever. He loves this job, and he only has time off for Christmas with his family in Melbourne."

"I'll miss you at Christmas." Derrek reached out to her.

She looked at him, "I can't go to Australia for Christmas."

Derrek shrugged, "Before you make that decision, why not give it a try this week?"

Lori shook her head, "I need to take a shower." She glided toward the bathroom, before turning around, "Maybe the two of you should take that advice." She disappeared into the bathroom.

I knew she was right. We could feel things out this week, while we were together. Could we do it? Could we sneak around and be together and have Lori and Derrek's parents be none the wiser? I certainly hoped we could.

There was a long silence, aside from the shower head running and whatever Lori thought singing was. Derrek was the first to speak. "I think it's best we don't."

Not what I wanted to hear, but the fear of getting caught and outed was too much for him. I looked at him and nodded, "Last night never almost happened."

"Agreed." He started to head toward the door. "I should try to at least make peace with Steph."

The thought of him going back to her at all hurt. But I knew he needed to. It was more complicated than your average break-up. It was a full-on divorce and separation of things, there was a child they had to think about. The logistics of us making anything happen seemed impossible.

He turned back around, took my hand, and looked into my eyes, "We're going to make this work, I just need to figure all of this out first."

That made me feel better. He wanted me the way I wanted him. It was a dream come true. I watched him leave and glanced over at the bag I bought last night.

I sat on the bed and thought about the things I could do to make things work with Derrek. I could see a future with him. I loved the idea that he already came with a baby, and if Steph could get on board, we would be a kick-ass group of co-parents. We would be those couples that would show up at all the sports games together. His two dads and his mom, and maybe a third dad if Steph ever met someone.

The more I thought about it, the more I wanted it. Maybe if

Steph, Derrek, and I all sat down together, we could all make this so easy, or at least as easy as divorce could be. I headed to Steph and Derrek's stateroom and knocked on the door.

Derrek answered and smiled, "Hey."

"Look, if the three of us sit down, we can figure this out. I like Steph, and Steph likes me. You and I can work. Can you imagine how kickass our co-parenting will be?" I was practically out of breath from excitement.

"I love that you want to do that, but Steph isn't here," Derrek told me.

"She's not?" This was trouble.

"No." He sensed it too.

I pushed through the door and kissed him.

He pulled me fully into his stateroom and closed the door.

My back slammed against the closed door as Derrek's lips pressed against mine. I wrapped my hands around his hips and his hands grasped my face.

Derrek pushed his tongue into my mouth, and they danced together as I pushed him to the bed.

I was determined this time. What I've wanted, without fully realizing it, for years was finally in my grasp. Energy surged through my body as Derrek's hand slid down my elastic waistband and grabbed my cock.

He rubbed my cock gently as we continued kissing.

I pulled away and sat on the bed gazing at the beautiful man in front of me. I pulled my shorts off showing my fully erect member. I pulled my wallet out. I had stuffed a condom in it earlier just in case.

"No falling asleep this time." Derrek's voice was low and gruff. He rushed to the bathroom and returned with a bottle of aloe and a smirk.

I wasn't sure how he wanted to take this, so I reached for him, pulled his trunks off, and took him inside my mouth. I used my hand to grasp the shaft and sucked on his head.

"Oh fuck." Derrek threw his head back. He held my head in his hands seemingly trying to grasp at my hair only to find that my short curly hair wasn't enough to grab.

It almost made me chuckle, but I had a task at hand. I wanted to make him cum. I focused on his pleasure and only his pleasure.

Derrek's knees started to shake as he let out a grunt and released into my mouth. "Oh God!"

I looked into his eyes as I swallowed his juices and wiped my mouth. "You taste good." I stood and kissed him again.

Derrek bit his bottom lip and he seemed to be trembling.

"You, okay?" I grabbed his shoulders gently.

"Does it hurt?" He asked.

"If you don't wanna do this, we don't have to, you know that, right?" I knew it would be his first time with a man, and I was always used to being the one on top.

Derrek nodded, "I know." The pause that followed his statement felt like an eternity, "I want to."

"Are you sure?" I didn't want him to feel pressured. "If all you're ready for is head." I was cut off by Derrek's lips kissing mine and his hand working on my cock again. He broke the kiss and moved his face next to my ear. He then whispered, "I told you, I want to."

I smiled and grabbed him by the shoulders again, this time with more force. I pushed him to the bed. I liked taking force with men, especially ones that turn me on as much as Derrek. I grabbed my cock and started to rub it.

Derrek reached back and moved my hand away as he continued stroking my dick.

I reached under him and did the same for his member. His groans made me extra horny. I wanted to suck him off. I pulled away and flipped him to his stomach. I wrapped my mouth around him and massaged my tongue on the head as I moved it deeper into my mouth.

Derrek moaned louder and louder as I continued to give him head. His hands massaged my head. It was clear he was used to someone with long hair being down there as he grasped at hair that was barely there. He released into my mouth with a loud "fuck!"

I looked up at him and smiled, proud of what I had accomplished. I reached for the box of condoms. I ripped it open with my teeth and wrapped it over my throbbing cock. I grabbed the aloe and poured it on my cock as well as around his asshole. I put some on my finger and moved it into his asshole. I massaged around inside of him with my finger for a few minutes. I worked a second finger into his ass. I moved in and out smoothly with the two fingers, then I was able to slip a third into him. I provided the same movement until I asked him, "Ready?"

Derrek nodded and raised his ass a little off of the bed.

I knew I had to take this slow. I knew it was going to feel uncomfortable, or even hurt. I gently pushed into him. I stopped every time I noticed Derrek winced. I continued after a few moments. I continued a few rounds like that until I was fully inside. "You, okay?" I ran my hands up and down his back to comfort any tension he had.

Derrek nodded with a slight wince.

I started pumping, slowly at first.

Derrek's wincing after a few thrusts into him started to fade and he started moaning and grunting. "Fuck, I had no idea this could feel so good."

I smiled and took that as the go-ahead to move a little faster. I wrapped my right hand around his right shoulder as I moved my hips fluidly and faster. I then placed my left hand on his other shoulder and managed to get to my normal speed while fucking.

"Oh, God." He kept chanting.

My body started to heat up and my cock started throbbing. Derrek's walls closed in around me. I was getting close, but I wanted this to last. "Oh, God." I wanted him to orgasm one last time before I exploded. I want him to have all the pleasure, I wanted his first experience with a man to be mind-blowing.

"Fuck, Ryan." His body started shaking under me. He let out another "Fuck!"

I knew I was good, so I pounded him until I released into the condom. "Fuck!" I fell on top of him, both of us sweating. I rolled off Derrek, took him into my arms, and kissed him.

"Holy shit, I had no idea how good that could be." He snuggled into me.

I kissed his forehead and squeezed him tight. I had no idea what the real world was going to have in store for us, but for now, he was mine.

CHAPTER 13

LORI

I turned the water on nice and hot, just the way I like it. The night with Justin played over and over in my head. I hadn't felt this way about anyone in a long time. I wanted to spend more time with him.

Then the anxiety started to creep its way through my head. The thought that I might have been one of his conquests of the summer. The thought that I was feeling real things for someone I barely knew. The thought that at the end of the week, I might miss him.

I lathered up my hair with the shampoo, I wanted to cry. I felt my heart breaking. I wanted him, but I knew it would never work. I was able to finally rest my heart rate when I reminded myself that he could be nothing more than a fling. I finished my shower and dried off. I grabbed my makeup and started to apply it as the mirror began to clear from the fog.

I emerged from the bathroom, totally made up and ready to hit the ship. I rummaged around my drawer in the dresser and found a pair of jean short shorts and a white halter top. As I slid into my halter top, I heard a knock on the door.

"Who is it?" I called out.

"Room service." It was a very fake-sounding woman's voice.

I casually made my way to the door, for the first time I was feeling uncomfortable on the ship. I peered through the peephole and saw Justin on the other end. I smiled, straightened out my clothes, took a deep breath, and opened the door. "Hey."

He was shocked, "You look great." He kissed me on the lips as he walked into my room.

"I thought you weren't allowed in our part of the ship when you're off duty?" I closed the door behind him.

He shifted his eyes back and forth, then he whispered, "I snuck out." I hit him on his chest, "Come on, it's not like they post guards all over the place. If I'm dressed in normal clothes and don't get recognized, I'm good." He slid on a pair of sunglasses and put on the worst American southern accent, "Let's hit the promenade young lady."

I laughed, "Americans don't sound like that." I slightly pushed and walked past him.

"That's how you all sound to me." I knew he was kidding, but I couldn't help but be playfully annoyed.

"And all of you sound like the Crocodile Hunter." I shot back.

He placed his hand on his heart like he was injured, "Oh, how dare you." He looked back at me, "He's a national treasure and from a different part of the country."

"He was a world treasure, and I'm from Minnesota, not Alabama." I explained.

"Oh right, your accent is that movie, what's it called?" I knew what movie he was talking about.

"Minnesotans rarely talk like that," I informed him, "especially around the Twin Cities."

"Twin Cities?" It never occurred to me that the Twin Cities were not known around the world. "There's a town called Twin Cities? Wow, and I thought towns in Australia sounded weird."

"They aren't a town; they are literally two cities. It's what we call Minneapolis and Saint Paul." I handed him a cup of coffee. I figured it was best to not go down the rabbit hole of what was originally considered the "Twin Cities."

He took it, "Thank you. So, which one are you from? Minneapolis or Saint Paul?" He took a sip, "Ooo, this needs milk."

"You a milk guy?" I handed him a few creamers, "And neither, I'm from a suburb, called Burnsville."

"I am absolutely a cream guy. Anyone who drinks black coffee is a sociopath." He poured cream into his coffee, "Burnsville, sounds like a nice town."

I nodded, "It's alright." I enjoyed growing up in Burnsville, close enough to the cities to enjoy sports games, but far enough away to feel like I was in a smaller town. "I'm glad to be out of Minnesota though."

"Considering what you told me about how cold it gets, I can imagine."

I grabbed my mug, smiled, and sipped out of it, "What do you wanna do today? My side of the ship, maybe," I offered.

"Your side of the ship sounds great."

"No kissing, you are just a new family friend." I noticed the confusion on his face. "My parents saw us last night and decided to tell Ryan that I was cheating on him. He made up a story that the three of us hit it off and are now friends."

"Your life seems too complicated." He seemed to be backing out of our fling, I wasn't about to let that happen.

"Not complicated. We just gotta sneak around a little extra when we're on my side of the ship." I moved closer to him. I wanted to kiss him again, like we did last night.

"I like being sneaky." He put his face very close to mine.

My heart rate went up. I felt like it was going to explode. With every breath he took that washed over my face, my muscles tightened longing for him. I wasn't ready but at the same time, I wanted nothing more. I kissed him.

Later, after our second make-out session, we decided to take a walk down the promenade. We walked side by side, no touching. People who didn't know us would think we were just an old married couple, and the people who did know me would think we were just two friends hanging out. Hopefully, we would run into Ryan and Derrek to make this even easier to avoid the drama of our family.

"How long have you been working on this ship?" I asked.

"This ship, the last four years." He looked out at the ocean, "This is our second season out in the Caribbean."

"You said something about an Australia cruise before?" recalling our first conversation, barely.

"Yeah, it started in Sydney, went out and around New Zealand."

"I'm so jealous of you growing up in such a cool exotic place." I had always viewed Australia as this exotic land that people didn't live in, they just talked about.

"Not so exotic, I mean, I guess there are places that are, but Melbourne is like any other city in the world.

"But it has kangaroos." I have no idea why the idea of seeing a kangaroo jump around like we see white-tailed deer in Minnesota was so intriguing to me.

"Kangaroos are also tasty." He has eaten a kangaroo? I didn't even realize that was a thing people in Australia ate.

"Ew."

"Not ew, they are delicious and pretty nutritious." He explained.

"I guess it's not all that crazy. I've had venison and gator." It took me a few minutes to realize that there is a lot more than your average beef, poultry, and pork that I've eaten.

"Deer meat, that's another good one." He likes his meat. "Have you ever had wagyu beef?"

"No?" I hadn't even heard of it.

"It originated in Japan, but is also highly farmed in Australia, if you ever go, give it a try." He pointed to a bar, "Wanna get a drink?"

"Hell yeah," we headed to the bar.

He peered over the menu then handed it to me, "What would you like?" He put on a more neutral-sounding American accent. It sounded much better than his super fake-sounding Southern accent he had put on before. I looked at him, what was I doing? Was I falling for someone that I could never have a long meaningful relationship with?

"Uh, a perfect margarita." I smiled at the bartender and glanced back at Justin.

With his sunglasses on, and that accent, even I wouldn't know who he was. "And I'll take the same."

"The accent?" I whispered as the bartender walked away.

"I used to do a little acting as a teenager, I had to learn how to do an American accent for a show I was in." He answered. "How's it sound?"

"Almost perfect."

"Good thing I didn't have to throw in slang." He let out a little chuckle.

The bartender returned with our drinks, and we took them to the outskirts of the pool, as far as you can go with glass.

"Must be cool to live like this." I started to envision what life would be like with Justin. Would I visit him and get free trips on the boat? Would I get some sort of job on the ship too? If I did, what would I do? I stopped myself, no no, this is just a fling. I couldn't throw my life away for him.

"Remember, I don't live like this, I work like this." He took a sip of his margarita.

"Right. Sorry." I looked up at the clear sky. "You ever thought about giving it all up and trying something new?" I wanted to know what chance I had with him outside of this fling.

"No, I've never thought about it." Not what I wanted to hear.

"What would make you wanna give it up?" Still fishing for the right answer, or at least my selfish right answer.

"I don't know." He kissed me on the side of my head, "I like hanging out with you." Not exactly what I wanted to hear, but it was close enough, for now.

"So, you said you did some acting?" I wanted to get to know him better.

"Yeah, a lot of television shows are filmed in Melbourne."

"Anything I would have heard of?"

He laughed, "No, I can't think of a single Australian show that has ever been broadcast to Americans. We Australians keep to ourselves."

"That's too bad, I'd love to see a little kid version of you doing an American accent." I mocked him. I did want to see this illusive show, "May be worth a trip to Australia sometime."

"I was in my final year of senior secondary, not exactly a little kid. I think Americans call it being a senior." He shook his head, looking embarrassed, "Besides, it's not worth a trip to Australia, there are a lot of other things to see that are a lot cooler than our terrible show." He was not proud of what he did. "Have you never been to Australia?"

I shook my head, "Nope, just Canada, Mexico, the Caribbean, and the UK."

"Then Australia itself is worth seeing, just to see giant spiders, the most venomous snake in the world, and egg-laying venomous mammals."

"Australia sounds awful."

"Huntsman spiders aren't even that dangerous to humans." I didn't care, I had heard about their spiders as large as dinner plates.

"So, wait, egg-laying mammal, I'm assuming that's a platypus, they're venomous?" That was something I didn't know about them.

"Well, we have the only two egg-laying mammals, echidnas also lay eggs." He knew a lot about animals out in his home country. "But yes, it's the platypus."

"They're venomous?" I had no idea until that moment, "That was not something they taught us in science class in America."

"They taught us about all of that."

"Well, you have to worry about killer animals."

"We do have the deadliest animals" He raised his glass, "To my home country."

I clinked his glass with mine, "Never going."

He laughed, "It's not that bad. Especially in the larger cities. Most of the dangerous stuff is in the outback."

"How close are you to the outback?" I rested my arms on the railing looking out over the pool. I peered over to this Australian. This hot man is from one of the most exotic places I could think of. I imagined him killing giant spiders and walking through a bunch of snakes that could kill him in minutes with their venom like Indiana Jones. What could be sexier?

He looked at me, "Don't worry, you'd be safe in Melbourne, it's hours away."

"Gotcha." I wanted him and wondered if he craved me as much as I did him. If our make-out session was any clue, then I was venturing to say yes, but I had no idea. "Do you like the States?"

He thought for a few moments before turning to me and asking, "Why do you all hate public transportation so much?"

"Some cities are great at it, but as for being a country, we are more into just doing it ourselves. Basically, I don't know the answer to that question." I admit to being part of that problem. I drove everywhere, and public transit had a strange stigma attached to it, at least where I was from. I know in cities like New York, it's a normal mode of transportation, and maybe it should be that way all over the country.

"Lori!" Ryan called out from the pool. I guess he and Derrek decided to go for a swim. He emerged from the water with my brother, grabbed towels, and came to the other side of the glass fence.

"Hey guys, how's your day been?" I asked.

The smiles across both of their faces were very telling. "It's been great." Ryan grabbed the drink from my hand and took a sip.

"You two working stuff out?"

Ryan had a very sheepish grin on his face when he said, "Things are going great."

I didn't want to think about my best friend and baby brother hooking up, but I knew that face anywhere. "Did you two…"

Ryan nodded.

I wasn't sure if I should celebrate or be grossed out. It was my baby brother after all.

"So, we're new friends, yeah?" Justin started as he gazed around, "Anything I should know in case we run into her family?"

"Too late." I noticed my nieces and nephew running a whole meter in front of their parents toward us.

"Auntie Lori!" they called out.

"Guys!" I held out my arms as the girls collapsed into them for a hug.

Grant stood a few feet back with a smile, "Hey." I honestly wondered when he got to be too cool for his Auntie.

"Grant." The girls' grips loosened. I turned to face him. "No hugs?"

Grant simply shook his head. "I'm not in a hugging mood."

"Alright." I hated watching my nephew growing up. I missed the little kid who would sit on my lap as he watched me build in The Sims.

"Ready to start another fight?" My passive-aggressive sister decided to blurt out the second she walked up to me.

"What the hell, Kasey?" Derrek stood between me and our sister.

"Don't get me started on you, family abandoner." I guess my sister hates both of us now.

"How'd you find out about me and Steph?" Derrek's voice was low, but still had an aggressive tone to it.

"After she kicked you out last night. She came to our room sobbing. Talking about you two getting a divorce." Kasey glared at Derrek.

"Leaving her for a dude," Dave added.

Derrek seemed panicked. He shook his head as his face turned red with anger. "I'm not leaving her for anyone, I'm leaving her because I am not happy." He took a deep breath, "I love her very much. I'm just tired of living a lie. I'm ready to be me, finally."

I was proud of him; I could feel my face beaming as I watched him stand up to Kasey and her husband.

Derrek was always a quiet kid, he never stood up for himself. He was bullied a lot in school, and it was up to me to protect him. As he got older, he and I just became so close, and I continued to protect him. He was quite angry with me when I left for California, but by then he knew Steph. We reconciled a few months after I left. In the time that I had been gone, he had learned how to take care of himself. I guess he had to.

"You can't leave your baby behind." Kasey stayed on the attack.

"He's not happy. Do you want him to stay unhappy his whole life? Not exploring a side of himself that he never felt like he could explore?" I decided to step up and help. I knew he could take care of himself now, but I was not going to let the two of them bully him into staying in a marriage that wasn't fulfilling him anymore.

Kasey looked at me, "Hey, selfish, you stay out of this."

"What exactly am I being selfish about?" I had heard it many times from my friends who had children. It's selfish of me to not want children. Selfish toward my future husband, selfish toward the overall plan for people that God created, and selfish that I want to have my freedom. It was a common theme in the world of parents toward people who had the audacity to live child-free.

"You and I have had this conversation before. You could settle down with a family, but you just want to go out, travel, party, and live your self-indulgent life." She was starting to sound just like our mother, and I hated it.

I started to walk away, "I am so glad that I got out of Minnesota."

"Yet another selfish decision you made." Kasey shot at me.

"What, it's selfish that I decided to start my career and excelled at it?" How could my going off and having a career be selfish?

"Do you even know what you did to this family when you ran away from us?"

I was shocked that she would say that I ran away. They all knew that, especially then, I needed to go to where the work was. I had a dream that I wanted to chase, and I wasn't going to let anyone make me feel guilty about that. I glanced at Derrek who just looked away, what was I missing? What didn't I know? "Okay, you have my attention."

"Mom fell apart, Dad started drinking a lot, the kids cried for months, and Derrek could barely take care of himself."

"I did alright," Derrek argued.

"You were a mess." I wasn't sure if Kasey was trying to just make me feel guilty, or if there was any truth to what she was saying.

"Maybe we shouldn't be doing this in front of the kids," I mentioned.

Kasey's attention was back on me. "You didn't seem to mind ruining their first night on the ship."

I wanted to argue. I wanted to fight back. I wanted to tell her that she was wrong, but she wasn't. I *did* ruin the first night here. Sure, my mother was at fault as well, but I didn't have to let her get to me. I should have just taken deep breaths like my therapist always tells me. I guess I am still that little kid who's desperately begging for her mother's approval. Not for who she wants me to be, but who I am and what I want.

I turned to the kids, "Guys, I am so sorry for the way I acted the other night." I was honest and genuine. I wanted to find everyone in earshot that night and apologize. Honestly, I considered rushing the stage at one of the big night shows, grabbing the mic, and doing just that.

"Why should you apologize?" Justin finally chimed in. He had been quiet this entire time, looking very uncomfortable.

"Excuse me?" Kasey looked at the blonde Aussie. "Who are you anyway?"

"The guy that Derrek's leaving Steph for?" Dave seemed to be stuck on this Derrek-liking-men thing.

"I'm a friend," is all Justin said. "I met her and Ryan that night. The night when she was completely broken because your mother was emotionally abusive. She's not the one that should apologize here." Justin took a step forward. "Your mother probably owes an apology to all three of you." He blurted out.

I had never been so turned on. I had never had a boyfriend stand up for me like this to my family. I had one tell my mother once that he would change my mind about children one day. Did I just say, boyfriend? No, no no.

"You have no right to get in the middle of this," Kasey fired back.

"You're right, but I am also not going to just sit here and watch you attack two of my friends. Lori is far from selfish, she's amazing, and maybe one day she'll believe that despite how you all treat her."

My heart started to race as I heard his words. It felt like my heart was going to beat right out of my chest. Then I felt it, I felt myself wanting to advocate for who I am and what I want out of life. I turned to Kasey, "You know what, you're the one that's selfish." I finally blurted out. "You and Mom expect me to live my life in Minnesota. But not only do you want that, you want me to be miserable, married, barefoot, and pregnant. I am so happy doing what I'm doing." I told her.

Justin placed his hand on the small of my back, it was the most comforting touch I had ever felt in my life. I turned to him and felt guilty. This wasn't a great way to be introduced to my family, not that we were going anywhere beyond this fling on the ship.

"I'm sorry about this." I whispered to him. I knew things with my sister were not going to get better. I knew we needed to get out of this situation before it got worse. Why was Steph doing this? Why was Steph trying to cause so much trouble? I wanted to blame it on her hormones, but that didn't excuse her for causing this much trouble. "Let's just go." I was done, I wanted to cry, but I wasn't going to do it in front of them.

Ryan, Derrek, Justin, and I left the pool area and headed back to the stateroom. When we entered the room, we all took a collective deep breath. My deep breath was more like me trying to fight back the tears. I hated this. I hated Kasey, I hated my mom, I hated everything. I collapsed onto the bed. Justin's hand on my back again helped. The bed moved slightly as he sat next to me and simply rubbed.

"I can't believe her!" Derrek yelled as he slammed the stateroom door shut. "I want to have a word with Steph about all of this."

"Not right now, mate." Justin stood and grabbed his shoulders, remaining calm. "You're way too angry to talk to anyone sensibly." Justin was right, talking to Steph right now wouldn't do anything but cause more fighting. "Look, talking to her about sharing your dirty laundry is something you two should sit down and talk about, but only when you've calmed down."

We heard the horn of the ship coming into port at Grand Cayman.

"Maybe a couple of hours off this ship is what we need." I propped my head up off the bed to breathe.

Justin shook his head, "I can't leave the ship." He looked back at my brother, "You three go have fun."

"You sure?" I asked.

Justin nodded, "I gotta get ready for my shift anyway," he started to make his way to the door, "I'll see you later, back on the ship? I'm slinging until two a.m."

I smiled and nodded, "Also, I'm sorry about my family."

"Everyone's family has crazy moments." He pulled me close and kissed me on the forehead. "I'll see you later."

"Later." We all said in near unison.

After Justin left, I turned back to Ryan and Derrek, "Alright. Ready for a day off this damn ship?" I asked.

"Yes, it'll be like Jamaica with the three of us just forgetting all our problems." It sounded like Derrek was calming down already.

"How about the two of you hit the island together, and I take Steph out and talk to her before you do." I figured it was the best thing for everyone, those two could connect and I could work on Steph before Derrek got his chance.

Derrek seemed uncomfortable with the idea, but he nodded, "If that's what you wanna do." He said.

"I think it's best." I placed my hand on his shoulder.

CHAPTER 14

LORI

I knocked on Steph and Derrek's stateroom door, and Steph peeked out. "Sorry, Derrek's not here." She seemed so broken.

"Steph, I'm here to see you." I might have been irritated with her for outing Derrek to Kasey and Dave, but I also wanted to talk to her and lessen the blow for when Derrek let her have it. I had to play nice, at least for today.

"Why?" She opened the door more, "I figured you and your brother would side with each other."

I would always side with Derrek. There was no question about that, but I needed her to trust and talk to me. "There are no sides between us." There was also this part of me that wanted our relationship to stay strong so when everything blew over and we all forgave each other, Steph and I could stay friends. She was family, and that would never change.

"You do know keeping your secret is gonna be harder right?" She fully opened the door and placed her hands on her hips.

"What do you mean?"

"Derrek and Ryan are gonna end up together. Your idiot brother asked me to move to California so he could try things with Ryan." She finally invited me in as she stepped to the side to allow me to enter.

I walked into an identical stateroom, just backward. "And you said?" I figured it was a stupid question, but I wanted to know everything that happened so I could start to figure out how to put out this fire.

"I wanted to punch him in the face!" Her hurt was clear. "You don't ask your soon-to-be ex-wife to uproot her life so that you can pursue a new relationship."

I held back a laugh at the thought that Derrek had the audacity to have that conversation now. "I get that."

"So, no sides? How does your brother feel about that?" she asked.

I shrugged, "He knows I came here to talk to you." I knew that if it came down to me defending my brother, I would pick him. However, I also knew they were choosing to bring a new life into the world, and their parents needed to be at least civil. I knew it wasn't my place to make sure that happened, but I also felt like it was my duty since I brought Ryan, "We're friends, and I don't want that to change."

"You thought that nothing was gonna change between us?" She sat on the bed and looked at me like I was an idiot.

"What is going on between you and my brother is your business, not mine."

Steph was silent for a few moments before she finally said, "You're right." She hugged me, "I figured you'd think I was a bitch."

After being attacked by my sister and her family, I kind of did. I also thought it was wrong for her to out him, and I wasn't going to let her get away with it. I gently said, "I just wish you wouldn't have spread it across the family."

She took a step back from me. "I didn't tell your parents, just you and your sister."

"You didn't think it would get back to my parents? And you outed my brother." That's what I was most angry about.

"When I was asked why we were splitting up, what was I supposed to say?" She didn't get that outing someone was a low thing to do.

"He wasn't telling us for a reason. Believe me, if he felt like it was the right time, don't you think I would have been the first person he would tell?" I wanted her to get it. "You could have said that you had grown apart."

"That would have been a lie."

"Outing someone is wrong." I decided to stand firm on that and wasn't going to budge. "What if the reason he didn't say anything was due to safety?"

"But it's not, no one will hurt him for it." Steph argued back.

"Whether someone would hurt him or not isn't the point." I shot back. I took a deep breath to try to remain calm and gentle. "The point is, it's not your news or story to tell."

"See? You are taking his side." I could see how she would think that, but I was taking the side of everyone who was outed before it was their time, before they were ready.

"No, what you did was wrong." I shook my head, "Look, let's just go out like we always used to, obviously sans alcohol for you." I held out my hands and grabbed hers, "I'm not kidding, I want us to stay friends."

She pulled away from me. "You think I'm a bitch." She didn't get the point I was trying to make.

"No, I think you're a wonderful person who's hurt, and through your hurt, you made a poor choice."

She smiled and nodded. "I'm sorry I outed Derrek."

"You need to say that to him." I placed my hands on her shoulders. "Especially if it got back to my parents. Telling your parents that you're gay, bi, pan, however, he identifies, is an important moment."

She looked guilty. "You're right. I am a bitch." She glanced out the sliding glass door, "And I can't even drink all my problems away like I normally do with you."

"No, but we can find another way to drown your sorrows. Let's get out on the land and find something to do."

Steph nodded. "Let's do it."

We looked at some things to do in Georgetown. "I know we can snorkel here. See some stingrays?" I asked her.

"Sounds like a blast." She half smiled through the brokenness that she had been feeling this whole trip. The brokenness was only growing in her. I wished I could take away everyone's pain from all of this.

"Then let's have some fun." I stood up. "Change into your cutest suit and meet me at my stateroom, yeah?"

Steph nodded.

I left to get changed into my favorite bikini, Steph and I were going to destroy Georgetown. That's what we always called it when we would go out drinking, we were "destroying the city." We couldn't drink, or at least, she couldn't, but we could still have a great time.

I grabbed my bikini; it had a light blue base and darker blue zig-zags across it. I slipped into it and grabbed a sarong that I had gotten on a trip to Mexico about six months ago. I wrapped it around my waist and slipped on my flip-flops. I skipped into the bathroom; I loved the way I felt in this bikini. I grabbed one of my hair ties and put my hair up into a ponytail.

There was a knock on my door.

"Steph?" I called from the bathroom.

"Yeah." Her muffled voice came from the other side of the state-room door.

I ran to the door and opened it for her. "Hey, come on in."

"One bed," She noticed. "How's that for sleeping?"

"It's not like we haven't shared a bed before." I started packing my beach bag with some clothes for later, a sweatshirt in case it got cold, sunscreen, and some other emergency essentials including my wallet.

"I guess your parents wouldn't have gotten two beds for a couple."

"It was a surprise to me, they've always been so" I put on a very sarcastic high-pitched sound, "wait till marriage" back to my normal voice, "kind of parents."

She nodded. "I accidentally slipped in front of them that I had a pregnancy scare before Derrek and I were even engaged, and they lost their shit."

We both laughed.

"Maybe they want me to have kids so bad, they don't care if I'm married anymore," I joked.

"So, you're never gonna want kids?"

I shook my head. "I never say never, but if I did, I would probably foster kids and then adopt them if things worked out."

"That sounds amazing." She paused, "Have you ever said that to your mom?"

"No, because it probably won't happen." I paused, "I remember a time when the daughter of a friend of hers adopted a little three-year-old and Mom said it wasn't a real grandchild for her friend." My mother was one of the most toxic people I know, but this family still flocks around her like she's this amazing woman. I never understood why.

"I can't imagine how hard it is for you."

"It sucks, I will never be good enough for my mother." I grabbed my beach bag, "Let's get off this ship." To be honest, this was the worst vacation I had ever taken, minus meeting Justin. "Seriously, let's go." I shook my head. I didn't need to be thinking about my fling, thinking about my fling meant falling in love, and that was not something I needed.

We left the ship and started our onshore excursion. We first headed to a beach to go snorkeling. There was a place not far from the port, it was within walking distance, and we were paying to go out for a little swim with some stingrays.

"I did this last time we were out here; it was great. The water is so clear." It was the coolest thing I had done, other than go skydiving. You feel like you're one with nature when you're swimming through that clear water seeing all the animals, having them not be afraid of you. "You ready?"

Steph hadn't been on one of these trips with us, she hadn't been outside of Minnesota other than the surrounding states, provinces, and of course seeing me in California. "I'm a little freaked, I've never done this in the ocean, just in a lake."

"Well, this is clearer than any lake you will find in Minnesota, trust me." I handed her goggles and a snorkel. "Maybe one day, I'll take you scuba diving." I raised my eyebrows a couple of times.

"Isn't that what they are having classes for while we're at sea and the damn pool is closed?"

I nodded, "Yeah, you gotta take some classes, nothing too crazy."

"Maybe I'll do that then."

"You can't while pregnant. Just come out to California after the baby comes and we can go take some lessons." I told her.

"You think I should move out to California too, don't you?" She asked.

"I mean, selfishly, I'd love to have you closer." Of course, I wanted her to move out to California. I would love it if Kasey and Dave did too. I hated being so far away from my nieces and nephew. Steph had also become so sister-like to me, I almost loved her more than my *actual* sister.

"And that's the only thing?" She questioned.

I looked down at the sand, "Okay, so I think he and Ryan would work well together. Is that so terrible?" She knew that he was attracted to men, and he wanted to experience that part of his life.

"It would be terrible." She told me. "All of this is just so hard."

"We aren't talking about this; we are going snorkeling." I wanted to keep her mind off everything that was causing her stress. I wanted her to come swimming in the ocean with me.

"You got it." She smiled.

We headed to the snorkeling spot and started moving into the water. As we waded, she turned to me and said, "I'll think about it, but don't tell them." She put the goggles on, and her mouthpiece hung on the side of her face, "I want him to be happy, I love him." She stuffed the mouthpiece in and slipped under the water.

I smiled and celebrated a little before following her into the water. I looked around for some animals to swim with, I saw a stingray and swam up to it. I moved my hand across its smooth body. I saw a school of fish off to the side, so I decided to follow them for a little while.

There were about a dozen of us snorkeling through this clear water. I saw some little corals and just looked at their beauty. There was always this part of me that thought I would have loved studying marine biology. I loved nature, always have, and always will.

After about an hour of swimming with some fish and stingrays, Steph and I were toweling off talking about our experiences.

"I saw you petting that stingray, they freak me out. Aren't they dangerous?" Steph seemed very impressed.

I shook my head, "No, they leave you alone unless you provoke them." We grew up in a world where Steve Irwin was killed by one of them when we were super young.

"Still, did he get you?" She asked as she looked me over.

I laughed, "Come on, let's go get men to hit on us at the beach." It was time for her to remember how great being single can be.

"I feel so bloated, I don't think any guy would even dream of hitting on me." Steph put her hands on her stomach.

"Oh please! You're incredible!" I shouted for the whole beach to hear. I spent years working on accepting my body for the way it looked. Now it was my duty to make sure everyone felt good about their bodies. All bodies are beautiful.

We found a spot with an unused umbrella. I'm not much for sunbathing, and Steph couldn't overheat. We laid our beach towels under the umbrella and sat together.

"I am truly sorry," Steph said to me as she opened the book she was reading.

"I'm not the one you owe an apology to." I reminded her. "You *need* to talk to Derrek." I looked out at the ocean. I could see the ship off in the distance and my mind wandered to Justin. The words I said to Steph earlier rang in my head, *let's go get hit on.* I suddenly felt like I was cheating or wanting to cheat on him. This wasn't good, and I knew it.

CHAPTER 15

RYAN

Derrek and I were going to spend the day on the island as our first real date experience. "So, where should we go?"

"To Hell." Derrek answered.

I was confused, "Excuse me?"

"It's a place here." Derrek said as he approached me and gave me a peck on the lips.

It felt good to get a kiss, but I was also aware that someone might see us. "We still have to be careful. Unless we three want to sit down and finally come clean about everything."

The nervousness was clear on his face, "You're right. Let's get out of George Town and then we can be a couple."

Unless his parents also wanted to visit this Hell place. I nodded, "Yeah, you're right."

We signed up for a tour shuttle and I just hoped his parents weren't on the same tour. At least the shuttle rides we could feel like a couple if they weren't around. We got on the shuttle and there was no sign of his parents.

Derrek leaned in and kissed my cheek. "My parents aren't here, so you're my boyfriend."

Boyfriend? We hadn't started using terms like that yet, but I wasn't opposed to it. "So, why do they call this place Hell?" I had assumed that there was a reason, that it wasn't just a coincidence.

"Oh, you'll see." Derrek told me as he grabbed my hand.

I felt his fingers interlace with mine and our hands rested on his lap. It felt good, having someone who cares about you is better than the little hookups I had done since I broke up with Vince.

I glanced over at Derrek. He seemed nervous and uncomfortable. Everything he ever thought about himself had turned upside down. He was abandoning his whole life and possibly upsetting his already abrasive mother.

"It's gonna be okay." I whispered to him.

"I hope so." He took my hand and squeezed it. Our fingers intertwined with each other, this felt right.

"Welcome to hell." Our bus driver said through the speakers on the bus. His voice was trying to sound menacing but also comical.

"We're here!" Derrek sounded like a little kid as he looked out the window.

"We're passing by the school of Hell." The bus driver pointed off to the side of the bus. He continued to make jokes about everything we saw in the town before we finally made our stop. "We have arrived ..." he said followed by slight maniacal laughter.

We exited the shuttle, and I did a quick glance.

"My parents aren't here." Derrek was clearly also looking as he tightened his grip on my hand.

I was happy he wanted to keep holding me. I was still nervous that we would have to do long distance, but he was at least worth giving it a try. Unless Lori could work some magic on Steph today and see if she can plant some seeds about them both moving to California.

We stepped onto the observation pathways over these pillars of limestone. "Wow."

"Yeah, isn't it cool?" Derrek pointed off to the distance. "It continues about half a football field."

It was beautiful, but also haunting. I heard our guide talking off in the distance. I pulled Derrek closer to hear more about this place.

"These are corals, so all of this used to be underwater." He explained as he gestured to the large black porous rocks.

"This all used to be a coral reef?" I asked Derrek.

"I guess so. I didn't pay much attention when I was a kid." He looked around in amazement as well.

I looked closer and I was able to see water hanging out between the rocks, "There's still water."

"That is from rainwater." The guide explained.

"That makes sense." I felt Derrek rest his head on my shoulder. I then rested my head on his head. "This is nice." I whispered to him.

We visited the gift shops and each bought something that advised that we had been to Hell and back.

The next stop on our tour was a turtle farm. We stepped off our shuttle for the second time, feeling more comfortable that we wouldn't run into his family at all so much so that we were now hand in hand.

The building was bright and colorful, there was something about the Caribbean that made everything seem bright. There was a mural of a sea turtle on the side as we ventured into the farm.

We saw a large tank and approached it. Inside we saw massive sea turtles. I had been to aquariums before, but this was like nothing else. They were incredible.

I tried counting how many were in that tank, I counted more than a dozen before some disappeared into the depths and others emerged.

"They're amazing." Derrek still sounded like the little kid that had been here before. It was fun to see it for the first time for me, but I also loved seeing it through his eyes.

After our visit with the turtles, we decided to take a stroll. We had another twenty minutes before we needed to get back on our tour bus.

"Wow, look at that!" I saw a little tiny lizard running around. It was great to see the wildlife that existed on these islands. Don't get me wrong, I live in California, so I have seen my fair share of wild lizards. I just think the high of being in a new place and this new relationship I was hoping to start, I felt like everything was new and exciting.

As we walked the trails, we passed by pools of water that

people were snorkeling in. I had kind of wished we had not taken the tour so we could have done some snorkeling, but I knew we still had one more stop before ending this trip. We stopped at one of the pools and just watched the marine fish swim around.

"Look," Derrek said in an excited whisper.

My eyes followed to where he was pointing, but I didn't see anything. "What?"

"A little sea turtle is hiding in the rocks." He continued to point.

I stared harder and with a squint, then saw one of the rocks move a little. "Oh wow, you're right."

A snorkeler swam by and startled the little turtle, and it swam off into another part of the pool.

"We should do this again," Derrek told me.

"Yeah, we should." If things did work out the way I wanted them to, I would be happy to do this on every anniversary.

"What's California life like?" he asked.

I shrugged. "It rarely, if ever, gets below freezing in Los Angeles." I started, "I would venture to guess it rarely dips below fifty degrees on an average."

The shock on his face told me that he could never comprehend living in a place that didn't get cold. "Man, that sounds like a dream."

I nodded, "I was happy to give up the harshness of the East Coast."

"I always visited warm places in the wintertime, so it just seems bizarre to have that be where someone *lives*." He looked back out at the water to watch the fish.

"But when you're somewhere that's constantly warm, you can go to a cold place for vacation." I knew that sounded bizarre, but it was nice to go somewhere cool sometimes. "Your sister and I like to go to Big Bear on our off-season to go skiing."

"Do you like skiing?" Derrek asked.

I nodded; skiing was one of the only winter events I enjoyed doing. I was also pretty good at it. "I was scared to do it when I was a kid, but once I understood how to control myself on skis, I ended up loving it."

We continued on our little adventure through the farm and came across what looked to be nursery tanks. There were people wading in the water and seeming to be playing with the baby turtles.

"Next time, we should budget more time to do some of these cool things," Derrek told me.

I nodded as I peered down at my watch and realized we had to start heading back to the shuttle.

We got back on our shuttle to head back to the city. Along the way, Derrek and I remained holding hands, our fingers interlaced, and his head resting on my shoulder. I was living this dream I had had for years. I knew the dream had to come to an end soon. Since we were returning to, not only his family but our big lie.

"So," I was worried about asking the question. I didn't want him to feel rushed. Coming out to your family is a big deal. Not to mention this coming out involved a divorce and an unborn baby.

Derrek raised his head to make eye contact with me. "So?"

"I guess if we're going to be together. Do you have an idea of when you might tell your family?" I dated a closeted guy once, and it was the most frustrating and difficult relationship that I had ever been in.

His name was Jonny, we were freshmen in college, and he was only just starting to come to terms with his sexuality. I had been out since my sophomore year of high school. We would go on "study dates," but I was never a part of his real life. I remember one time when his family came to visit, he introduced me to his family as his friend.

The relationship ended because I just couldn't stay his dirty little secret. We stayed connected on social media afterward, and he never truly came to terms with his sexuality because his parents would never have accepted him. He's still single and I see random pictures of his "friends" on these social media platforms. I genuinely feel bad for him.

I just didn't want that to happen with Derrek. I wanted him to be in a place where we could be together.

Derrek looked out the window of the shuttle and said, "I haven't thought about that."

That worried me, I couldn't get connected to another guy who would never fully live his life. I wanted an authentic relationship.

"Can I have time?" he asked.

I wanted to afford him time because I know it can be difficult, but being closeted makes relationships complicated. I liked him, so I swallowed my worry and simply said, "Take all the time you need."

Derrek smiled and put his head back on my shoulder as we continued our way back to Georgetown.

I just soaked in these moments. These hidden moments would become a lot easier when he comes to see me in Los Angeles, and hopefully moved there.

"So, would I live with you and Lori when I move out there?" he asked nervously.

"I think that's a conversation you should have with her." I knew he was worried about affordability, "It *is* expensive, so just keep that in mind," I explained to him.

"Maybe if Steph and I work it out enough, we could be friends and be roommates. Get a three-bedroom?"

A three-bedroom? He had no idea what it was like to live in Los Angeles. "You're looking at over five thousand dollars in rent if you're planning on living *in* Los Angeles for a three-bedroom," I told him.

"That's insane," Derrek yelled loud enough for everyone on the bus to hear him.

I knew that it was devastating to hear. The truth was, he was going to have to move to the outskirts of the city for a three-bedroom to even be a little affordable.

"Encino is pretty affordable." I thought out loud. During traffic, the commute between us would suck, but at least it was doable. "You could find something closer to three thousand for rent there." I wanted to offer he just come live with me. Lori and I had a loft in our condo that could be his bedroom until we were ready to truly live together. But I figured, living together even if we weren't *living* together, was a big step and would only ruin this relationship.

"Encino," he said to himself.

I squeezed his hand. "Talk to Lori, maybe she would be willing to let you live with us until you can figure out your own place, or things get more serious with us." I wanted him to know that I planned on asking him to live with me, just not today.

Derrek snuggled in more with me. "I just hope Steph can accept all of these changes and come with me to California."

I think we both knew that he would never leave that baby. Steph not going to California meant that we would never truly be together. It was devastating.

CHAPTER 16
LORI

Steph and I got tired of sitting at the beach, she had finished her book and I felt like I was trying to cheat on a guy that I had dated once and kissed twice. He wasn't even my boyfriend.

"You, okay?" Steph was so attuned to people's emotions.

I looked at her and shrugged. But I guess I could be honest with her; she was in on the lie. "I met someone."

"Why did you bring Ryan and not him?" Steph was excited. She bounced and her curly red hair bounced with her.

"I met him on the ship," I admitted.

She looked at me. "Wait, you met him on the ship?" She shook her head in disbelief, "How can you even know that he's someone you want to be with? You met him when? A day ago?"

"We met the night I stormed out of dinner," I admitted. "We spent the day with him in Jamaica, and I was with him last night."

She gave me a jokingly judgmental look, "You were *with* him?" She asked, hinting at us hooking up.

I shook my head, "Don't get excited, we made out in a pool, but that's as far as it went." I left out the part about my craving for more.

"What if your parents saw you?" She panicked.

I shook my head. "He's part of the crew and we were in the

crew area of the ship." I paused. "But they did see us walking arm in arm last night, I guess."

Steph's eyes widened. "They did?"

"But Ryan explained to them that he's a friend we met and had made plans with, but he *wasn't feeling well* last night."

Steph nodded. "Good." She got excited again. "Tell me about him and when do I get to meet him?"

We were getting off-topic, the point of us hanging out today was to get her ready for a conversation with Derrek. "He's Australian, has shoulder-length blonde hair and he is so sexy."

"He's your dream man."

I had always told everyone that one day I was going to pack up and go to Australia to find a man. "He looks like he should be on the cover of romance books." I told her. "I think I'm starting to like him." It felt good to finally say that out loud. I looked down at my feet for a few moments before they drifted back up to meet Steph's gaze, "I wanted to come to the beach to find someone else to hit on to try to get my mind off of Justin, but I felt like I was trying to cheat."

"Then tell him how you feel. He clearly likes you." Steph grabbed my hand in hers and squeezed it.

"There are a lot of complications. He loves working on this ship and he may have a girl he hooks up with on every cruise," I told her.

"What's a relationship without a little complication?" she told me. "You deserve to be with someone that makes you happy." She stopped and started to tear up.

"What?" I asked her.

She shook her head and walked away from me. "Nothing."

I wasn't going to let her do that. I walked up to her, "What?"

"Everyone deserves to be with someone that makes them happy." She said, "Derrek hasn't been happy for a long time."

"Have you been?" I had never asked her that.

She shook her head, "I think we both were just swept up in the idea of getting married." She admitted. She then turned to me, "I even had an emotional affair once." Guilt streamed across her face as her words fought to stay hidden.

I was taken aback, "When?"

"Last year," She told me, "He's this guy at my office, he's all the things I love about Derrek, but…"

"Straight?" I joked.

She nodded, "Not exactly what I was going to say, but that too." She laughed through her tears, "I was going to say sportier." She was always someone who enjoyed a beer at a baseball game.

Derrek was never into sports. He played a couple in high school and was good at them, but he never liked watching them. He still plays basketball occasionally, and goes to the gym, but other than that, you wouldn't catch him going to a Vikings or Rams game any time soon.

"What happened?" I asked her. She called it an emotional affair, so I assumed nothing physical happened.

"We flirt in general at work a lot, but last year, things got a little heavier. I started having dreams about him." She explained.

"Like *dreams*?" I asked.

She nodded, "I would wake up and look over at Derrek and be disappointed that it wasn't Greg." She admitted. "I even started making plans on leaving Derrek once to be with him. And that's when I realized I needed to figure things out. I decided to stay with Derrek because it was easier."

I felt bad for her, and for Derrek. Neither of them was happy in their marriage and now they were going to have a baby that would either have grown up in a loveless marriage or a broken home.

"I know, I probably need a lot of therapy." She moved away from me, still filled with guilt. "I was obsessively holding on to a marriage that I wasn't happy in. So obsessed that I got pregnant to coerce Derrek to not come to terms with his sexuality or at least stay with me while coming to terms with it."

I grabbed her by the shoulders and pulled her in for a hug. "Thank you for admitting that to me." I loved Steph, she had always been one of my best friends since Derrek and her started dating.

"I have to stop holding him back" She melted into our hug. "If Ryan is going to make him happy, then he needs to be with Ryan."

"Are things still a possibility with this Greg guy?" I asked.

"Not if I'm moving to California." She seemed disappointed.

"How likely is that?" I tried to hide my excitement that it seemed like maybe she was warming up to the idea.

She looked at me, "We had talked about the idea of it years ago, but we kept putting it off. So, yeah, eventually, I think it's worth going out there."

I wanted to tell her that finding a man out there would be impossible, so she should go with the Greg guy but then thought how much more complicated it would be having three adult lives to move out there so my brother and best friend could be together. "So, you're feeling better about all of this?"

She shook her head, "This all still hurts like hell, but I also know I can't be selfish."

"It isn't selfish. Derrek loves you; he always has, and he always will. You know that." I told her, "You were doing what you do in a marriage, trying to make it work, sans the trying to trap him with a baby maybe."

She nodded, slightly embarrassed, "Yeah, not my best moment." She placed her hand on her belly and said, "We did want kids. It's not like this was a total surprise or something we didn't want."

I never thought that she would ultimately change their lives for something neither of them wanted. "I never thought that." I reassured her.

She took a deep breath, "Let's go do something fun."

I smiled and took her by the arm, "Let's go." That's when we saw Ryan and Derrek get off of a shuttle.

They were holding hands until they stepped off the shuttle. They immediately let go of each other as they looked around.

"Ready to face it?" I asked her as we approached the boys.

"As ready as I'll ever be." Steph reluctantly followed me.

"Hey, ladies." The awkwardness was palpable as Ryan raised his hand.

"Hi." Steph stood next to me, her hands behind her back.

"How's your day been?" Derrek approached Steph and reached for her.

Steph backed away a little, "I'm not sure what's appropriate anymore." She told him.

"We can still hug." Derrek's voice was soft and comforting. It was clear from his face that he loved her deeply and wanted them to remain close. He was hurting too, I just hoped Steph saw that.

I nudged her with my shoulder and gave her a look. "It would be nice if the four of us could remain close friends like we always have been."

"I'd like that too." Ryan interjected.

Steph shot him a look that could kill.

"Apparently, I'm not part of this conversation." Ryan walked away from the group.

I pulled Steph aside. "You said you wanted Derrek to be happy," I reminded her.

"I know but seeing them together just sent me spiraling." She looked over to Ryan who was gazing over some trinkets through the display window of a store "I should apologize."

She headed to where he was shopping while I kept a respectful distance.

Derrek approached me. "Think those two will ever be, okay?" His urgency made his desperation clear. He wanted peace between the people he cared about most, he always had.

"I hope so." I wasn't sure how this was all going to pan out in the end. "I told her about Justin."

Derrek turned his focus on me. "That was stupid."

"Why? She knows that Ryan and I aren't together, and she's been planning on keeping my secret." I knew there was a slight chance that she might go rogue again and out him to Mom and Dad, but she said she regretted doing that with me and Kasey.

"The fewer people that know about this whole thing the better." Derrek crossed his arms and turned away.

I decided to probe the idea of Derrek telling the family about everything before they heard it from Kasey or Dave if they hadn't already. "Is it the worst thing in the world for them to find out about all of this?"

Derrek's face morphed into one of shock back at me. "You're falling for Aussie boy, aren't you?"

I was silent. I didn't want to admit that I was falling for him, I couldn't even admit it to myself. It had become clear on the island that yes; this was more than just a hookup for me.

Derrek groaned. "You can't."

I knew that my exploring feelings with Justin was not only possibly going to ruin my secret, but Derrek's too. "You're right." It was disappointing but risking outing him to my parents wasn't worth trying things with Justin. There will always be more hot romance book cover Australians in my future, right? "I won't see him tonight."

"Thank you." Derrek let out an exasperated sigh as he hugged me.

Ryan and Steph walked up to us, seemingly to be on friendly terms.

"You two work everything out?" I asked.

Steph nodded, "Yeah, I'm going to try harder to be good about this."

Derrek took Steph by the hands and smiled at her, "Steph, I love you. I do. That will never change."

She smiled at him and pulled him in for a deep hug.

Later, we had all gotten back on the ship and had dinner with each other, this dinner was uneventful as my dad kept my mom drinking white wine to loosen her up. Ryan and Derrek had decided to go gambling at the casino, Steph went to bed since she wasn't feeling well, and I was doing everything I could to stay away from Justin's bar. Not only was it risking all of our secrets, but how would this work? There was no way I could start a relationship with someone who doesn't even live on dry land, and when he does it's in another country.

I walked around the deck of the ship, it was getting late, and I didn't even realize it until I was grabbed and pulled around the corner. I was pushed against the wall and Justin's lips were pressed against mine.

After our kiss, he gazed into my eyes. "I missed you tonight," he whispered.

I pushed him off me a little. "We can't," I told him as I started to walk away.

"Did I do something to upset you?"

I turned to him. "My parents saw us last night. They thought I was cheating on my 'fiancé.'"

He had to understand the ramifications of us being together. "Sorry, I just like you."

I knew I had to get out of this relationship, flirtmance, whatever the hell it was. I went to my one fear, that deep down inside I knew wasn't true. I looked down at my feet, I couldn't even look him in the eyes when I asked, "Do you do this a lot?"

"Do what?"

"Pick up girls and date them each week?"

"I've never done this. I usually keep to myself." He held out his hand and took mine in it, "There's something about you."

I wasn't one to believe in love at first sight, but lust on the other hand, that I believed happened in an instant. I couldn't look at him, I needed to get out of there before I made the worst mistake my heart could make. That lust I felt for him, which is all it could have been, was stronger than ever. I needed him inside me. I knew if I stayed, I would let it happen. I finally looked at him.

He leaned again and we kissed.

I pulled away, "There's more at stake than my fake engagement."

"Your brother."

I nodded. The energy between us could light up a city. I wanted him, I wanted him to kiss me again, I wanted him to take me to his sardine can of a room and have me, I wanted him to take all my worries away, I wanted to run away with him.

He started walking away.

"Justin," I called out as tears flooded my eyes blurring my vision.

"It's okay, I got it." He disappeared around the corner.

I wondered if I hadn't lied this whole time, would tonight have looked different? I felt a tear fall down my cheek. My heart was breaking, I couldn't understand why, we only met a few days ago, and we would only have a few days left together before we parted ways and never saw each other again. What was the point? I turned and headed back to the room.

CHAPTER 17

RYAN

After dinner, Steph headed back to the room and Lori wanted to be alone. Derrek and I finally had some alone time again. I had told everyone that Derrek and I wanted to go gamble, but I wanted alone time with him. We headed back to my and Lori's stateroom so that there was no chance that his parents would see us being together. I wasn't sure what to expect. We slept together once so far, but I wasn't sure if it was just a spur-of-the-moment thing like when we almost did the night before, or if he was ready to jump into a sexual relationship. I was prepared either way.

We entered the room with a bottle of wine. I grabbed a couple of coffee mugs and said, "Sorry, this is all we have in here." I placed them down on the table next to the bed.

Derrek smiled and said, "It's okay." He poured a little wine for both of us. He seemed nervous.

"I'm not expecting anything," I wanted to reassure him that tonight could be just us together, that just because we had sex once before, I wasn't expecting it again.

"Let's go out on the balcony." He motioned to the sliding glass door.

It was a simple way to be outside overlooking the ocean without getting outed. Even if his parents were outside on their balcony, they were on the other side of the ship. Only strangers would see us. I followed him outside and rested in the two chairs with our sacrilegious mugs of wine.

"Today was so great." Derrek said as he stared out at the ocean.

"Yeah, I haven't had a day like today in a long time." I missed having a boyfriend. I forgot how great it was to have someone to come home to. "I want more days like this." I felt Derrek's hand on mine, and I looked at him.

"We will." His smile was sweet and sexy.

I knew he meant well; I knew he wanted the same things I did, but I still worried about his hesitation to come out to his family. I didn't want to push him to do it, but I still wanted to urge him that life is easier once everything is out in the open.

We sat and looked out at the ocean at the moon and stars as we held hands and drank our wine.

Once the bottle was finished, we stood on the balcony. I held him in my arms, and I pressed my lips against his. It was the most romantic kiss I had ever experienced. A little liquored up, out on the ocean in the Caribbean, with a man that I had wanted to kiss for years. Here he was, mine. I could feel myself getting excited. I wanted to pull him to the bed, but I wanted him to make the decision.

Our kiss ended and he walked back into the stateroom. He poked his head through the door and asked, "Are you coming?"

I smiled and followed him inside.

As I stepped inside the room, he had already taken off his shirt and started working on his pants.

I pulled off my shirt and grabbed the box of condoms and aloe vera.

He rubbed his hands on my chest, which just got me even more excited.

I smiled and kissed him. This time more passionate and with a destination. I pushed my tongue deep into his mouth and our tongues began to dance between our mouths. I pushed my shorts down to the floor and stepped out of them. I felt Derrek's hand on me. He gently stroked my member and I let out a groan as he did it.

Derrek then wrapped his arms around me leaving me wanting, no needing, more.

I pushed him down to the bed and we continued to kiss. My body temperature rose as sweat beads formed all over. This was better than before. Our first time was great, but something about this was so much hotter. Maybe it was my fear of his first time and disappointing him, which I didn't. This time, we both knew what to expect.

I kissed his neck and down his chest. I placed my tongue between his pecs and teasingly licked all the way back up to meet his mouth once again.

Derrek's hands massaged my back outlining my muscles. His touch almost tickled. His breath was hot and heavy. His erect cock pressed into me.

I moved down his body again and took him into my mouth. I held the base of his cock with my hand and rubbed as my mouth and tongue worked on the head.

Derrek groaned as he threw his hands against his face, "Fuck!" He called out in pure pleasure.

I continued this motion until he released into my mouth. I let go and swallowed the cum in my mouth.

Derrek was speechless, his eyes closed and the look of heaven upon his face. I kissed him one more time before flipping him over. I rolled the condom over myself followed by a lot of aloe.

Derrek looked back at me with a big smile, ready for me to enter just like I had before.

I slipped two fingers into his ass and started moving them in and out as I had before.

"Ryan." Derrek seemed to plead.

I smiled and dropped down on top of him and slowly slipped into him. It felt so good. I watched his face to make sure he was okay. This was only his second experience with this kind of sex, and I wanted him to enjoy it.

Derrek winced a little as I entered him.

"You, okay?" I asked.

"Yeah, I'm good."

I carefully thrust my hips against him while keeping my eyes on Derrek's face. I began upping the tempo of my thrusting.

"That's it." Derrek's face molded into that of pleasure. His front half collapsed to the bed.

I lowered my stance and kissed the back of his neck as he moaned.

Derrek's moans grew louder and louder letting me know that I was doing this right. "Faster," he pleaded through bated breath. I knew he was coming closer to an orgasm.

I also felt myself reaching climax. I slowed my speed to help keep myself from finishing so quickly. I was caught up in who I was with and how much he wanted this.

"Why'd you slow down?"

I put my mouth near his ear, "I want this to last." I whispered in his ear followed by sucking on his lobe which evolved into kissing his neck.

"Shit…" He started to call out. He was close.

The thought of him close to finishing made me more excited. I decided there was no stopping it now. I started my tempo faster and faster.

"Oh, God!" Derrek called out in orgasm. "Fuck!"

I pumped a few more times when I released into the rubber around me and fell on top of Derrek, "Oh my, God." I had never felt so good before. That was by far the most exciting sexual experience I had ever had. I was on such a high I was close to telling him that I loved him. I knew it was too soon, but after that, what else is there to say?

I rolled off Derrek and we lay there, still catching our breath.

"That was amazing!" Derrek exclaimed.

I smiled smugly to myself at his words.

Derrek rolled over to his back and snuggled in with me. He placed his hand on my chest and ran his hands up and down. "I had no idea sex could feel that good." He outlined my sweaty pecs with his finger

I wrapped my arm around Derrek and squeezed him.

There were no more words that needed to be spoken, we just lay there, and I could have been there forever with him.

A few moments later, there was a knock at the door, "Who is it?" I glanced at the clock, it was midnight, who would be knocking at this hour?

"Kasey." Lori and Derrek's older sister was at the door.

Derrek shot out of bed, "shit." He whispered in haste to me as he dashed out of the bed and started getting dressed.

"What do you want?" I asked.

"I need to talk to Lori," Kasey was starting to sound frustrated.

"She's not here, she's…" What could I say? I looked at Derrek, "With the Aussie?" I mouthed to him.

"Better not be." He mouthed back with anger in his face.

What happened? Why was he against her dating the Aussie on board, as long as they were careful? "On a walk."

"At midnight?" Kasey seemed distressed.

I hopped out of bed and started getting dressed as well.

"Look, I just need to talk to her about the whole Derrek being gay thing." Kasey's mumbled voice seemed more distressed.

I glanced at Derrek whose face was a mix of confusion, fear, and anger, "She told Kasey?" Derrek whispered.

I shook my head, "Steph was off running her mouth." I admitted. I knew it would ruin a lot between him and Steph, possibly even with me for knowing. I just couldn't let him believe that Lori would out him like that. I made sure we were both fully dressed before opening the door, "Hey."

Kasey noticed Derrek in the background, "Derrek." She walked into the stateroom, "Is it true?"

Derrek was silent, tears starting to form in his eyes then nodded, "Yeah, we're getting divorced because I want to be true to myself and find fulfillment in my relationships. For me, that means with men. Well, one man." He said as he glanced up at me.

Our secret was slowly unraveling and now Kasey was going to know everything.

Kasey was confused and looked back at me, behind me she had

to have seen our sex paraphernalia. "Oh, my God." She turned to me, "Does Lori know?"

I nodded, "Yes, we aren't together. She brought me on this trip because she didn't want to face more crap with your mom, which she faced anyway."

"And you two?" Kasey's shock did not let up.

"We didn't plan any of this. Steph and I were already separating before the trip and things just evolved with me and Ryan." Derrek walked up to his sister and grabbed her shoulders. With pleading eyes, he begged, "Please don't tell Mom and Dad yet."

"Of course not." Kasey wrapped her arms around Derrek and through tears, she said, "I love you." She held her brother for minutes before letting go, "Does this make you happy?" Kasey asked.

Derrek looked at me. "Very."

"Then I'm happy for you." She looked between me and Derrek, "Does Steph know about all of this?"

Derrek nodded. "Yeah, we're trying to work on being okay with everything.

"So, tell me about this mystery boy that Lori's having an affair with?" She asked as she sat on the bed.

"His name is Justin, and he's a bartender on the ship." I sat next to Kasey.

"Does she like him?" Kasey asked.

Derrek sat on the other side, "She does, but I told her not to go for it."

"Why not?" I had been wondering about his 'She better not' words from a few minutes before.

"Because now she's ruining more than her secret, she would also ruin mine, and I'm just not ready to tell Mom and Dad about all of this just yet." Derrek was not getting any closer to wanting to say anything, even after our stay-in date we just had.

I was devastated. Not that I thought an incredible night together would make him magically ready, but for the way Kasey reacted to it, I thought maybe he would be okay too.

"Why not tell Mom and Dad? They would want you to be happy." Kasey placed her hand on his knee and squeezed.

"Because I don't want to disappoint them." Derrek's relationship with his parents seemed just like the relationship Lori had with them too.

"You won't disappoint them." Kasey placed her hand on Derrek's shoulder, "They want you and Lori to be happy, whatever that means."

Derrek shook his head, "No, you'll never get what it's like for the two of us." He stood and turned to face her, "You found the love of your life on your first shot, you got married at twenty, and had your first kid a year later." Derrek walked over to the sliding glass door and looked out at the night ocean sky, "You don't know what I went through after I broke up with that girl in high school, then got with Steph and Mom asked me every time we spoke when I was going to pop the question. When I finally did, then it was when were we going to have babies. Truth be told, I was coerced into proposing at all by Mom." He admitted. "I love Steph, and I always will, but at the end of the day, I used her to hide who I was."

"So, why continue to hide?" Kasey asked.

"Because I don't know how she'll react." Derrek turned back to face the bed that Kasey and I sat on.

"She'll be fine." Kasey seemed so sure, but it was clear to me that Kasey didn't experience the same trauma that Derrek and Lori had experienced.

I placed my hand on Kasey's shoulder, "Coming out is a very vulnerable thing to do, and it has to be done on your own time." I explained to her. "It's not like you bringing home your boyfriend. The default in our society is straight, so telling someone that you're not, isn't always easy." I looked at Derrek who had turned back around to look at me, "It's okay, I will be by your side when you're ready."

Kasey reached for Derrek. "So will I and Lori."

Derrek smiled. "Thanks."

Kasey nodded and walked over to her brother for another hug. She then left to go back to her room.

"Are you sure you're okay with us staying a secret a bit longer?" Derrek asked.

I nodded, "Of course." I took a deep breath, "Closeted relationships are difficult, but we'll make it through." I reassured him.

"I should head back to my room." Derrek said after a labored sigh, "I don't want to kick Lori out of her bed."

"Okay, have a good night." I kissed him. I wanted him to stay, but I also knew that it was important for him to do what was most comfortable for him.

The door closed behind him; I felt a slight tear form in my eye.

Kasey gently touched my shoulder, "He'll be okay."

I smiled and placed my hand on hers. How did their terrible mother raise such wonderful and affectionate children?

CHAPTER 18
LORI

reached the stateroom, tears streaming down my face. I forgot how much it hurt to feel your heartbreak. I forgot there was physical pain. I opened the door fearfully waiting to hear if there was any sex happening. When I didn't hear anything, I opened the door fully and walked in.

Ryan made his way out of the bathroom, "Hey." He must have noticed my tears, "What's going on?" He grabbed me and pulled me down to sit at the foot of the bed.

"I broke things off with Justin." I fell into his arms and sobbed. "I really liked him, Ryan."

"Then why did you break things off with him?" Ryan pulled me away to investigate my face.

"Because I don't want Mom and Dad to find out about the two of you." I told him.

"Look, Lori," Ryan started, "If you can't be with Justin out of fear that Derrek will get outed, then the same rule should apply to us."

It made sense. It was obvious that he was into men if Mom caught him kissing a boy. If she caught me kissing a boy that wasn't Ryan, it just meant that I was cheating, not that my brother was into guys.

"You deserve your relationship just as much as we do." Ryan's hand gently moved up and down my back.

Relationship? Did Ryan just say he was in a relationship with my brother? I smiled through my puffy eyes, "Relationship?"

Ryan nodded, "We're going to give this a real try, at least I hope."

"Hope?"

Ryan walked to the sliding glass door and opened it to let the air in, "I think Steph is going to be a huge predictor as to if this will work."

"Why Steph?"

"Well, Derrek doesn't want things to be awkward." Ryan started, "It would be one thing if he ended up dating a complete stranger to both of them."

I was confused, "Why would that make a difference?"

"Well, when Steph and I were making up on the island, she worried that we had had an affair or that this was planned. I told her that neither one of us expected this."

"She's one to talk." I blurted out. I knew it was a mistake the moment I said it, it wasn't my story to tell that she had had an emotional affair.

Ryan's eyes widened, "What?"

I shook my head, "nothing." I stood up and walked out onto the balcony.

"No no no, you know something." Ryan followed me.

I looked at him, "It's not up to me if other people know what Steph told me."

"She had an affair." Ryan started piecing things together, "That's why she would immediately jump to Derrek and I having an affair."

I shook my head, "No, she didn't have an actual affair." I knew there was no way out of this, "You can't tell Derrek, please let Steph do it in her own time."

Ryan nodded.

"She *did* have an emotional affair with a co-worker of hers. She even thought about leaving Derrek about a year ago because of the way he made her feel." I explained.

"So, nothing physical?"

I shook my head, "No, she wouldn't cheat on him."

"Good," Ryan looked out at the ocean. "I think you should go for it with the Aussie."

"I can't." I refused to put any of this in danger.

"Lori, you're crying over a guy that was supposed to be a hookup. There's something more there." Ryan had always looked out for me like a brother would do for his sister. Like I always did for Derrek. Ryan didn't talk to his own family all that much, so I guess I was it for him these days.

I did want to go find him and fix things, I wanted to explore why it felt like I needed him in my life. I just knew that if I did, and I got caught, everything would unravel. "I can't put Derrek, or you, in that situation."

"Lori, I'm out. I don't care if your parents know I'm gay." Ryan rested his hands on the bar overlooking the ocean. "You bringing your gay best friend to masquerade around as your fiancé is one thing. If your parents figure that out, it won't automatically reveal that Derrek and I are together." Ryan grabbed my hand, "I know Derrek is scared to be figured out. I don't want him to be outed any more than he already is. He isn't ready." He pulled me into a hug, "You finding love isn't going to mess anything up."

Love? That was a bit much.

Ryan pulled out of our hug and looked me in the eyes with both of his hands firmly holding my shoulders, "Go find that Australian model and fix this." Ryan demanded.

It still worried me, but that's what I wanted, "Tomorrow." I walked back into the stateroom, "Right now, I need sleep." I collapsed into the bed and drifted off to sleep.

The next morning, I woke up to the sound of Seagulls. I looked at the clock, "It's 11 am?" I sat up in bed. I never sleep this late.

The sliding glass door was open as a warm breeze blew across my face, "Did we land in Mexico?" I called out to Ryan.

He poked his head through the sliding glass door, "Yeah, about an hour ago."

"I don't sleep this late." I told him.

"Well, we didn't go to bed until like nearly 4 a.m., so it shouldn't be surprising." He reminded me.

"Is there coffee?"

"Of course, there's coffee." His head disappeared out of the stateroom again.

I climbed out of bed and grabbed some coffee and joined Ryan out on the Balcony, "Can you believe we're on the tail end of this adventure?"

"This is our last stop, right?" He asked.

I nodded, "Yup, tomorrow is a day at sea then back to Fort Lauderdale." I was a little disappointed. Aside from the first couple of days, my trip was pretty amazing. Time with my brother, which I never get, and I met an incredible guy that I was hoping to make things right today.

"I am going to miss this trip. It kind of makes you want to move down here." Ryan smiled as he watched dolphins jump in the distance.

I looked at him, "But what about your job?"

Ryan's gaze was filled with guilt, "I mean, if I can talk to you as a friend instead of my boss, I would tell you that my heart hasn't been in animation for a while." Ryan looked around at the people on the island, "Honestly, it took this trip for me to realize there are more important things in the world."

"Like love," I told him. I had no idea if this meant that I might lose my best background painter and best friend to love. "What do you want to do? As your best friend .."

Ryan peered back out at the scenery, "Depends on where Derrek ends up being."

I smiled and nodded, "You go wherever your heart is happy."

"It won't be happy in Minnesota winters, so if that's where we end up, there will be hell to pay." Ryan laughed.

I wanted to laugh as well, but I knew that it meant losing so much of what I held dear to me in California. I was hoping and praying that Steph would move out there.

Ryan and I met with Derrek and Steph, who were feeling better, to take a hiking trail. I peered around the groups of people hoping to see Justin like we did in Jamaica. I didn't see him.

"No Aussie?" Derrek asked.

I shook my head. "No." I knew it had to be said. I knew he'd worry about it or be angry with me, but I knew what I wanted, "I'm going for it."

"You can't." Derrek started to panic.

"Well, well well." I heard my mother's voice from behind me.

"Hey, Mom." I turned and threw her a fake smile.

Mom wasn't alone, behind her was the entire family. "I think it's about time we all spend time together." It was as if she was trying to make me feel guilty for choosing to spend days without her. As if my independence was somehow a threat to her.

"Of course." I choked out my words. Now, even if I did see Justin, I wouldn't be able to talk to him like I want to. I glanced at Derrek, who also seemed disappointed. There was no relationship talk on this adventure through some Mayan Ruins.

We got on a bus that took us to San Gervasio which was the Mayan Ruins on the island of Cozumel.

We passed through a gate and traveled partway into the jungle. The bus came to a stop as we departed and began seeing the start of some ruins.

"Hey, there's a map!" Grant yelled as he ran over to it.

I was not looking forward to being on this trek with my whole family, and I could only imagine how awkward all of this was for Derrek, Ryan, and Steph.

It was then that Justin emerged from the crowd. He had clearly come another way because he was not on the bus.

Our eyes met and I smiled. I approached him hoping he didn't run off.

His smile widened as I made my way over to him. He smoothed his shaggy blonde hair back, "Hey." He said meekly.

"Hi." I told him. I wanted to jump into his arms and kiss him, but I knew that I still had to play pretend until it made sense to tell my family the truth.

"We shouldn't be seen together." He turned away.

"Please come, spend the day with us." I felt terrible about how we ended things, and I wanted to fix it. I knew I couldn't fix it in the current climate, but maybe if Mom and Dad got to know him, it would be an easier transition of "This is who I am *actually* dating, sorry I lied."

"I shouldn't." He was clearly still hurt that I had broken off our … whatever it was we had.

"I'm going to tell them the truth." I admitted as I peered down at the ground.

He looked at me, "What about your brother?"

The more I thought about that situation the more I realized just how pathetic of an excuse it was for me to not be with Justin, "Because lying to my family about my relationship doesn't out my brother."

Justin smiled, "When do you plan on telling them?"

I wasn't sure. I wanted to tell them now. I wanted to take him by the hand and proclaim he was the one I wanted right this second. However, I also wanted to enjoy the day. "How about tonight? I will bring them to the bar, if you're working you can take a break to come hang out, and if you're not then meet us there." I looked back at Ryan, "I think Ryan is sick of this lie too." I just wanted out. It was a stupid idea from the beginning and things would be a lot less complicated if I had just come here alone.

"Deal." He told me, "I do work tonight, but I will certainly see what I can do about taking a few minutes." He took a step closer, "I usually wait a little while before meeting a girl's parents." He looked past me and over to my family.

I smiled at the idea that he was talking like this was going to be some long-term thing. I was still trying to figure out the logistics of him being out at sea most of the year, but I wanted it too.

I led Justin to our large family unit. "Everyone, I would like you to meet my friend Justin."

"Hello." He awkwardly waved.

I introduced him to everyone, except the people he already knew, and we started our hike.

My mother pulled me out of the group with a stern look on her face, "It's not appropriate to have male friends when you're in a relationship." Here she goes again, what is and isn't appropriate behavior for women.

"Why's that, Mom?" I knew I was not getting out of this lecture, so I figured I would dive right in rolling my eyes and all.

My mother's stern look turned full of anger. "Don't you dare roll your eyes at me, I don't like it when you have male friends at all. The only time a girl should be with a man on her own is if they are dating."

I stopped in my tracks, "We've had this same argument a thousand times. What about Sonya, in high school?" I snapped at her, "She's pansexual, can she not hang out with anyone?"

"Don't get snippy with me." She grabbed me by the arm and started pulling me with the group again, who had all noticed we were arguing.

"Do the same rules apply to men?" I liked arguing with her overly traditional ideals, mostly because they were unfounded, and she couldn't back them up with facts and statistics. She would often back herself into a corner and I would win the argument.

"Lori."

"Seriously, Mom, what about nonbinary people, can they hang out with men and women? Or is that based on who they're attracted to?" I never understood her thoughts on gender roles, especially as the world was changing, and the realization that gender is a social construct about how one should act based on the sex they were assigned at birth.

"There is just no talking sense into you." This was her normal reaction when I threw examples at her that she couldn't talk her way out of. "What happened to my little girl?"

"The little girl that was indoctrinated into purity culture?"

"What do you have against staying pure for your husband?"

She had done that, she never even kissed Dad until they were standing at the altar.

"Nothing, if that's what you genuinely want to do." I shrugged. "I simply want to live my life the way I want to live it." I was brought back to the fact that she ordered just one room for me and Ryan to share. She had always preached to wait until marriage to have sex. Dating was even looked down on when I was a kid. The idea of casual dating, that is. Did she assume Ryan and I have sex because we live together? Or does she think that sex isn't even an option for me until marriage so therefore me sharing a bed with a boy is safe? Was there a difference because I introduced Ryan as my fiancé instead of my boyfriend? I couldn't figure out what was happening anymore.

"I am letting you. I let you bring your boyfriend on this trip and live in sin as your nieces and nephew watch." She looked over to the group who were at a decent distance and now watching us. "At least there's a theoretical ring involved." She took a pause, "And that's another thing!"

"Oh, Lord." What was she having an issue with now?

"Where is your engagement ring? How are other men supposed to know you're spoken for without one?" She glanced back at the group, "Does he not make enough money to get you a ring?"

"Mom!" I shook my head. "I don't want to enable the wedding industry for being predatory. For guilting people into spending a shit ton of money in order to prove their love for one another. I don't need expensive jewelry."

"What is wrong with you?"

"What do you mean?" At this point, I wanted out of this situation.

"You don't like weddings now?"

"Weddings are fine, but they shouldn't cost tens of thousands of dollars!" I proclaimed.

"So, you're just going to live in sin?" She clearly missed the point.

"I am walking away from this conversation." One thing I had been learning from my therapist was setting boundaries, which I was terrible at with my mother. I had always wanted my mother to love me, and sometimes, I believed she did. I knew these feelings and beliefs were important to her, but the fact that she was basically requiring me to feel the same way was where I needed to draw that line, and I was finally at a breaking point with her. This conversation sent me over the edge.

"Don't walk away from me." She chased me down.

I turned to her and looked into her eyes, "If you want to be in my life, then you need to shape up." I told her, "You and I need to agree to disagree on gender roles, or else I can't have you in my life anymore." It was something I always wanted to say, but I never had the guts to do it.

I rejoined the group and we set off to look at the ruins.

Justin and I were able to separate from the group enough to have some alone time. He pulled me close as we looked around to make sure we were alone, he leaned in and kissed me. He put his mouth near my ear and whispered, "I want you."

I would have let him have me right there in front of the dozens of iguanas we had been seeing on this hike, but even I had some decorum. "How about tonight?" I whispered back with a seductive smile.

Justin nodded, "I will make sure my bunkmate is out of the room."

"Why not sneak to my side of the ship so we can have a nice comfy king?" I offered. "I can make sure Ryan is somewhere else." I wanted to take him back to the ship now. I kissed him again.

Justin's hands wrapped around the small of my back as our kiss intensified. It was clear, he was thinking the same thing.

I pulled away and told him, "Should we go back now?" my heart was racing so fast I felt like I was out of breath.

Justin nodded.

We walked back to the group, and I grabbed my stomach, "Hey, everyone, I don't know what I had for breakfast, but I am all of a sudden not feeling great. I think I'm gonna head back to the ship."

"Oh sweetheart, what's going on?" My mother pretended like

twenty minutes ago we hadn't had a fight over morals. It was gross that she could just pretend like nothing was wrong.

"Maybe she's pregnant," David said as he nudged Ryan.

"Definitely not." I laughed nervously.

"Look, I need to head back for my shift anyway, "I'll see to it that she gets back to the ship, and your stateroom safely, okay?" He played it up by speaking to Ryan.

"Thank you, I owe you." Ryan walked up to me, "You gonna be, okay?" He looked at me with concern.

I winked at him.

He gave me a knowing and loving smile, "Okay, you go back and get better." He decided to play it safe with our lie for the moment and gave me a peck on the lips.

"Thanks." I said as Justin guided me back toward the bus.

"You sure you're not gonna regret missing these ruins?" He asked.

I shook my head, "I've seen a lot of other ones, I climbed the pyramid at Chichen Itza right before they stopped letting people climb it." I admitted.

"How old were you?"

"I was fifteen." It was one of my proudest moments. "I was so out of breath by the time I got to the top, and my legs were so sore the rest of our trip."

We got on a bus heading back to the port. Justin felt comfortable enough to hold my hand on the trip back to the ship.

"So, do you want to come to my stateroom?" I rested my head on his shoulder. I had wanted this for days and it was finally happening.

"If you'll be more comfortable there, sure." He kissed the top of my head, "But we're forced to cuddle in my bunk."

I let out a little chuckle. Part of me thought it was a great idea to sneak back into the crew portion of the ship. I liked doing things that felt wrong sometimes. However, the thought of him and I getting up and standing out on the balcony together made it feel more romantic.

We reached the ship and I had decided to let him guide me to his bunk.

"My bunkmate is working right now, so we shouldn't be disturbed." He told me as we slipped past the employee-only door. He took my hand and guided me down to where his bunk room was.

The bunk room was so small two people could barely fit. "Wow." I said to him,

"Yeah, it's tough to get two people in here. But we're only here to sleep, so." He pulled me close, his hands on my hips and his deep blue eyes piercing into my soul.

I hadn't felt this turned on in a long time. Sex had become so casual to me since my last serious relationship ended. This felt different, this meant something. I was nervous.

Justin leaned in and kissed me.

I wrapped my arms around his neck as I melted into his deep passionate kiss. I opened my mouth just enough for his tongue to enter. He was an amazing kisser. I moaned to let him know just how good it felt.

His hands cupped my breasts over my shirt. He then moved his hands down my body and slid them under my shirt and bra. He ran his thumbs over my nipples as they grew harder.

I felt my clit tingle at the want and desire I felt. I moved my hand down his chest, feeling each and every muscle all the way down. I slid my hand down his pants and gently grabbed his already hard cock, he wasn't kidding when he said he wanted me. I rubbed his member as it hardened more.

Justin broke our kiss and pulled his t-shirt off revealing the chiseled abs I had felt, God he was sexy.

I pressed my hands against them and kissed his chest, then his neck, then back to his mouth. I backed away and removed my t-shirt revealing my bra. I was always nervous about undressing my size eighteen body in front of men. No matter how sexy I knew I was, it was always nerve-wracking that first time fully revealing myself. Justin held me close and kissed me again.

Justin's hands ran up my back as he unclasped my bra. I wriggled out of it and let it hit the floor beside us. He pulled his shorts down and they landed on the floor beside my bra.

I followed suit and slid my bike shorts and panties to the ground. I broke our kiss, "Which bed?" My heart was racing, I had never wanted anything more than this moment.

He smiled and pointed to the bottom bunk. "God, you're beautiful." He told me as he looked at my now fully naked body.

"So are you." I told him as I lowered myself onto his bunk. I grabbed his hips and pulled him closer. I grabbed his cock again and wrapped my mouth around his head. I sucked and licked the head as I rubbed the stalk.

Justin let out moans as his hands grasped my head and his fingers became tangled with my hair.

I loved giving him pleasure, I loved that he wanted me, I knew I was falling in love with him, but I didn't care. I wanted him. My mouth let go of his cock as I laid back in the bed ready for him.

Justin knelt down and grabbed my legs to hold them up. He placed his tongue on my clit and licked.

"Fuck." I was already so turned on by him that even the slight touch of his tongue on me and I was already being sent over the edge.

He slid one finger into my vagina and rubbed my G-Spot perfectly. His tongue still working my clit and his finger working my G-Spot, I couldn't contain it. I moaned and called out, "Fuck!" over and over again. Just then, he stopped.

I opened my eyes and made eye contact with him as he rose up from between my legs.

Justin joined me on the bed. He rested on me and kissed me again. His hands explored my body as he touched my breasts, and my belly, then started moving lower. He began kissing my neck and moved down to my breasts. He sucked on one of my nipples and used his fingers to play with my clit again.

My body quivered at his touch. My core warmed with anticipation of what was to come. I felt myself about to orgasm, but his touch stopped again. His version of foreplay was getting me to the edge and then pulling me back. It was slightly annoying, but it was doing the trick.

His lips pressed against mine again. His hands were playing with my hard nipples. I was over the foreplay. I reached down and started to massage him, if he was going to play games, then so was I.

Justin stopped kissing me and let out a groan. He looked around, "Condoms." He hopped out of bed and grabbed a box from a dresser drawer. He looked at me, "Always beneficial to have a roommate that tries to sleep with passengers and other crew members." He grabbed a package out of the box and started to open it.

"And you don't?" I didn't want to break the mood, but I also wanted to call him on his shit if he was going to call out his roommate for the thing he was doing at that moment.

He rolled the condom over himself and joined me back on the bed, "I don't, you're the first, and only." He told me and kissed me again. After the kiss, he said, "You're special, I like you a lot."

I wanted to believe that to be true. I wanted to believe that he had never slept with a passenger before. I smiled and said, "Then what are you waiting for?"

Justin plunged into me. My walls collapsed over him. He moved his hips fluidly as his cock filled my core.

I closed my eyes and threw my head back as his tempo picked up, "Yeah, that's it." I encouraged. "Faster." I pleaded.

He pumped his hips faster and faster.

I pulled his face to mine as we kissed, his hips not skipping a beat. His lips were wet from a combination of my juices and his sweat. He started to grunt as he moved faster.

I felt myself getting close, I wanted this so bad, "Harder" My voice was more a whisper now as I was so close to orgasming.

He obliged as his hips thrust with more force. He moved his hand down and played with my clit to intensify the orgasm I was nearing.

"Oh, God!" I chanted as my pleasure increased. My entire body started to tingle. I knew it was coming and it was going to be intense. I couldn't even make words anymore, I just moaned.

I knew I only had a few more days with him, and then we would never see each other again. This fling will have been flung. I wrapped my arms around Justin's chest with no intention of letting him go. I just wanted to stop time and let this be how we existed in time and space.

"You with me?" Justin was out of breath as he looked into my eyes. His pace slowed as his attention was on me.

"Yeah." I was able to break free from my brain and focus on Justin again. "This is good." The slowed-down pace brought my body down to allow for more time before I orgasmed, but I knew I was on the edge. One more fast couple of pumps and I would be gone.

Justin kissed me again as he began to pump faster and harder again. This time, he was going in for the kill. It was clear he was done playing games and was going to give me what we both wanted.

"Oh shit…" I chanted as I felt myself about to go over the edge. "Oh fuck!" I cried out just as my body exploded in pleasure. Every muscle in my body spasmed as I experienced the most intense orgasm I had ever had. "Oh, Justin!"

Justin smiled proudly as he continued to pump. His grunts had evolved into moans as he collapsed on top of me as he joined me on cloud nine.

"That…" I couldn't even put words to what I had experienced.

Justin rolled off me, sandwiching himself between me and the wall, "That was incredible." He was out of breath, and he ran his fingers over my exposed breasts.

"You said it." My heart was beating so hard I was afraid he could see my chest moving. I wasn't sure how to tell him that no man had been able to pleasure me like that before. I knew I needed to do that again before I left.

Justin kissed me and looked at me with a distinct sadness.

"What's wrong?" I asked.

"You leave in a few days." He told me.

It was nice to know we were thinking the same thing. It provided me relief that he didn't want me to go just as much as I wanted him to follow me off this ship. "I know." I told him.

We kissed again, knowing it was close to our last.

As we kissed, all I could think was how much I wanted to come clean about all of it to my family. I wanted to tell them that I had finally met someone that I could fall in love with, the only problem was, we were not going to be together in the end. We were destined to part, destined to be nothing more than a one-week affair.

CHAPTER 19

RYAN

We returned to the city after a couple of hours of hiking through the ruins.

"We should go swimming!" Lilly tugged on Kasey's arm pleading with her.

I was hoping to get some more alone time with Derrek since we only had a few days left together until we had to figure out how this would all work. I glanced at Derrek, who was already looking over to me.

Steph looked over to Derrek and told him, "I'm gonna go lay down."

Derrek nodded, "You rest up." He gave her a hug followed by a kiss on the forehead. He looked her in the eyes and said, "I *do* love you."

She nodded as her eyes started to well up. This was hard for her; we both knew it. It was one thing to separate from your spouse, let alone for your spouse to decide to explore their sexuality with someone else, someone you have looked at for a few years as a good friend.

I felt guilty. I knew I shouldn't, we were falling for each other and that wasn't my fault. If I could not fall in love with Derrek, I would have avoided it, but as they say, you can't help who you love.

"I'll walk back with you, sweetheart." Derrek's mom said as she too, looked miserably exhausted. "I have had it with this humidity." She wrapped her arm around Steph's shoulder as they guided each other back toward the pier.

"I guess I had better follow." Derrek's dad seemed exhausted by his wife's dramatics over the last week.

"I guess that means it's just us," Kasey said as she turned to me and Derrek. "Ready to hit the beach?"

" I'm kind of hungry." I placed my hand on my stomach. "I was thinking about hitting a restaurant in town." I looked at Derrek. "Wanna join me?"

"Since my sister left you high and dry, why not?" He smiled.

Kasey smirked and said, "Have fun, you too." She turned and walked away with her family.

"So, where do you want to go?" Derrek put his hand on my shoulder. "Ryan?" He tried to get my attention again.

I was lost in my thoughts, I didn't want to out Derrek, I wanted him to tell his family when he was ready. There had to be a reason why he wasn't saying anything yet.

"Ryan!" Derrek yelled one last time which finally got me out of my trance.

"What?" I asked.

"Where do you want to go for lunch?" He looked out at the streets of Cozumel.

I shrugged, "Let's go find a place."

"You, okay?"

No, I wasn't okay, I was terrified. This is why I refused to date guys in the closet anymore. It just made things too complicated. Then again, nothing about this situation was easy. I was playing straight, so I was pushed back into the closet. I was falling in love with my best friend's brother while my best friend, who is supposed to be my fiancé, is falling in love with a crew member that we won't even see again after this trip. I didn't want to burden Derrek with my worries, so I turned to him and said, "I'm fine."

We found a little family-owned restaurant that seemed to be dead compared to the big United States chains that we saw along our walk. It never ceases to amaze me how people from the States will still go somewhere they can go any time while they're visiting another country.

I looked over the menu and realized that my two years of high school Spanish did not stick around. "Oh boy."

"Yeah, maybe a chain would have been safer for ordering food." Derrek laughed, "I haven't taken a Spanish class since college."

"I haven't since high school and I'm two years older than you." I laughed.

"We're just a couple of dumb Americans, aren't we?" Derrek let out the cutest guttural laugh I had ever heard.

Our server came by, she was tall and thin. She wore her hair back in a high ponytail, "Hola." Her voice was perky.

"Hola" was pretty much the only Spanish I remembered. "Uhh, hablo ingles." I was able to reach that phrase deep in the recesses of my memory.

"Perfect, how can I help today?" Her voice still as perky as ever through her thick Mexican accent.

"Can we just get a couple of beers for now?" Derrek asked as he continued to glare at his menu.

The server left with a nod.

"I mean, I know what these dishes are, but I am not sure about the ingredients." I told Derrek as I pulled out my phone. "I guess this is where translation apps come in handy." I laughed. I turned on my app and hovered the camera over the menu as my app began to translate the ingredients.

"So, what do you want?" Derrek asked.

I looked at him and held back my desire to answer "You." I just smiled and said, "This Carnitas Huevos Rancheros sounds good."

"Cool, can I see what you have?" He reached for my phone, which I handed over. After a few minutes he simply said, "I think I want to just get a chicken tamale."

I smiled; it was nice to feel like we didn't have to sneak around. I just hoped that he would be ready to tell his family soon. I wanted to be proud of my new boyfriend. I blushed at the thought of even thinking that word. "What is this?" I wanted to know his thoughts on what we were doing.

There was a slight pause and Derrek cocked his head to the side, "Lunch?"

"No, us."

Another pause, "I thought it was pretty obvious." He reached for me, I accepted his hand, and we gripped each other, "You're my boyfriend."

I squeezed his hand and smiled.

There was another palpable pause between us when Derrek finally said, "I want to tell my family."

I was confused, he had never wanted to tell his family before, "That's a new development."

"I thought about it all day, and now here, being with you. I want this." He told me.

We enjoyed our lunch and held hands as we re-entered the ship. We had spent our lunch discussing how to tell his parents. We wanted to come clean with everything. I wanted to talk to Lori first.

"I'm gonna make sure that Lori is cool with coming clean, how about you go talk to Steph? We want everyone on board here." I told him.

Derrek nodded and headed toward the stateroom he shared with Steph as I headed toward the one I shared with Lori.

"Lori?" I asked as I poked my head into the stateroom door hoping to not find them in the act. The bed was made, and I saw Lori standing out on the balcony. She was leaning on the railing. I had known her long enough to know when the aura around her was somber. Something happened. I walked out to the balcony, "You, okay?"

"Yeah." I could hear her broken voice. She had been crying.

"Liar." I shut the sliding glass door and mirrored her by leaning on the railing.

She sniffed and wiped a tear from her cheek, "I'm falling in love, and it sucks." She told me.

I put my arm around her and pulled her in for a hug, "Can't you make something work?" My shirt was immediately wet from her tears as I heard her start to sob.

"How?"

I squeezed her tight. I kissed the top of her head. I wished I could take this pain away. I knew at least one thing we could do before the week was over and she could enjoy her last couple of days with Justin. "Your brother wants to come clean."

Lori pulled away a little, "About what?"

"All of it, the divorce, the fact that he's into men, our relationship." I was hoping Lori saw this as a sense of freedom, hoping that this would relieve her, even just a little.

"He wants to come out?" She put on her proud sister smile and sniffed again.

I nodded, "And he wants to tell your parents that we're boyfriends."

"That's amazing." She hugged me again, but this one felt different. It was full of excitement and tighter. "I'm so happy for you."

"Ready to break up?" I jokingly told her.

"Well, I cheated on you this afternoon, so, yes," She joked back. "How does Steph feel about all of this?"

"Derrek is talking to her now." I looked into her puffy eyes, "If you two are falling in love, you'll find a way to make it work." I told her.

She shook her head, "It's not possible."

"Sure, it is, you've proven your whole life that you can make anything possible if you try hard enough, and you know it." I got in her face to remind her of how incredible she truly was. "You are a warrior and always have been," I told her.

"What if I want off the battlefield? What if I want to stop fighting for everything I want?" She sounded so defeated.

"One more fight," I told her.

"Two." She shook her head and looked down at her feet. She must have seen the confusion in my face, "Telling Mom and Dad that the four of us have been lying the entire trip? That's going to be the thing that will make the captain finally toss all of us overboard as shark food."

I nodded, this was going to be a lot for her mother to take in, but I knew it was for the best. None of us liked lying to start with, but Lori had been living in survival mode with her mother since she started puberty and her mother started bugging her about finding a man. "We can handle it."

"I hope so." She looked at me, "Does he make you happy?"

I nodded, this week, since we had spent so much time together, I had never been happier. I wanted to spend every moment with him. I wanted to hold his hand and share our dishes at dinner. I wanted to kiss him in the hot tub. I wanted Lori to move in with Steph, so Derrek and I could spend the last two nights together.

"Then let's tell my parents." She said as she wiped away the last of her tears. "Let's go to their stateroom."

I followed Lori out of our stateroom as we headed toward where Steph and Derrek were staying.

"You can't do this to me!" I heard Steph's voice from the other side of the door.

"I guess Steph isn't on board." I hesitated to knock.

"Maybe we should wait," Lori offered.

Just then the door swung open and Steph, who had a murderous look on her face, said, "What?" While looking directly at me.

"I'm guessing you don't want to tell everyone," I told her.

"Weren't you the one who outed Derrek to me and Kasey?" Lori stopped her from moving forward, "What? All of a sudden you have a conscience about if he's ready to tell people about his sexuality when it comes to our parents?"

"Stay out of this," Steph told Lori as she pushed Lori out of the way. "Go ahead, tell your parents, I don't care!" She yelled back at us. "Marrying you ruined my life, Derrek!" She stormed off.

"Let me see if I can calm her down," Lori said as she ran off to follow Steph.

I turned to Derrek who was now crying. I walked up to him and hugged him, "Are you okay?" I asked.

He nodded, "Yeah, but she was so angry."

I didn't want to tell him that I understood her anger. This had to be difficult for her, just like it was difficult for us to be going through this. I said nothing, I just held him. I wanted him to feel like I was completely on his side, which I was, but I worried that even showing empathy to Steph would only upset him more. "It's going to be okay."

"I can't tell my parents until she's okay with it." He admitted.

I knew that was going to be the case. I knew that he still loved her. I wanted to help, but I knew this was something he had to face alone. He was in love with two people, he just wanted to explore his sexuality. "If you need to stay with her, you can." The words pierced my heart. I wanted him to be happy. And if being in the closet, or just being with her, until she was okay with all of this made him happier, I would learn to live with that.

Derrek was silent, it was terrifying. I didn't want to lose him now that we were together. Then he finally said, "I want to be with you." He pulled away to look at me, "I love her, I do. I always will, but I want to be with you. That's my choice."

I was thrilled that he wanted to be with me, even if it made him stressed out at the moment. I pulled him in for a kiss, without realizing the door to the stateroom was still wide open.

"What is this?" Leslie's voice pierced through my soul.

Derrek looked through the door. "Mom."

"Oh, my God." My heart was pounding and not in a good way.

CHAPTER 20
LORI

I caught up with Steph, "Can we talk?"

"About what?" Her eyes were puffy, her face was beat red, and she looked so stressed.

"Please, just sit." I pulled her over to a bench in the hallway.

She obliged and sat down next to me on the bench, "This is difficult for me too, you have to know that!" She cried out.

I nodded, "Of course, this is difficult for you."

"I had a whole life planned with Derrek. Now that whole life is shattered." She told me.

"It's not shattered. It's just going to look different." I pulled her in for a hug. She had been in my life for a long time, she *was* family. I didn't care about the legalities of her being my sister-in-law, she was my sister as much as Kasey was and I would defend that to anyone that questioned it. I hated the fact that this was destroying her.

"But he was supposed to be my partner for the rest of our lives. Until death do us part!" She reiterated the vows they took.

She wasn't seeing what I was trying to get through to her, "And he will be, just not in the way you thought." I looked down at her belly, "My little niece or nephew will have the coolest life if the three of you can learn how to do this together."

Steph was silent for a few moments as she grasped her belly. "I just don't want to do this alone."

"You won't trust me. There's no way Derrek would up and leave like that. Ryan would never let him, and you know my parents." I told her. I then paused, "And if you come to LA, I am always there if you need me. If not, then I'm just a plane ride away."

It seemed to relieve her that she wasn't going to be alone, "I guess three parents are better than one." She seemed so defeated at that moment. "But that doesn't make divorce or seeing your husband fall in love with a man easy."

"No, I'm not saying it's supposed to be or going to be." I stroked her back, "But you both deserve to be happy." I took a pause, "Even you said that you could tell he wasn't as happy as he could have been." I reminded her.

"But he was mine." She looked at me, "Do you know what it's like? Growing up feeling unloved, and then you get to feel it for the first time?"

I nodded.

"I just…" She started to cry.

I held her close again, "You deserve to be loved by someone who loves you back the way you *need* them to."

"But how do you fall out of love with the person that you planned on spending the rest of your life with?" This was an interesting question.

I had never been married, but I was close once before. I had been living with my first boyfriend, I didn't date until college. He and I had started a life together, but he ended up finding someone thinner and what I used to think was prettier. "Remember what you told me when Jay left?"

"That you should forget about his fatphobic ass, and that you're incredible and beautiful." She wiped a tear from her eye.

"You are incredible and beautiful. You deserve the world. Just because my brother wasn't the one, you two came together and are choosing to bring this beautiful life into the world."

Steph let out a little chuckle through her tears and looked at me,

"Thanks." I could see that she was only pretending to feel better. Nothing was going to make this okay for her. She was facing life alone for at least a while. "I just can't imagine going back into the dating realm, especially with a baby."

I thought about it for a few moments then rested my hand on her shoulder.

She looked at me, tears streaming down her face. "Thank you, really." She showed me a weak smile.

"You're going to be just fine, and I know this is hard." I wanted to urge her to support Derrek through this difficult time as well, but I realized she was in no way able to support anyone.

We hugged and sat together for a few more minutes until she dried her eyes and nodded as she said, "We need a drink." Her smile was stronger and more genuine.

I laughed, "I am *always* up for a drink." I stood and held out my arm for her to take so I could guide her to the bar.

We walked into the bar; Justin was there. Somehow, he was even more attractive to me now, now that I had seen him naked, and he had given me the best orgasm of my life. I felt my heart pounding, it took every ounce of willpower to not fly over the bar, tear off each other's clothes, and take him in front of everyone.

"Hey there, pretty lady." He winked at me.

His voice made me melt. "Hi," I gave him a flirty look.

Steph pulled on my arm and looked excited. It was good to see her in a better place. She gave me a knowing look, "You weren't feeling sick, were you?"

I shook my head, "Maybe a little lovesick?" I whispered back to her. I was a little embarrassed to admit it, but I truly liked this guy and our little hookup felt great. It was exactly what I needed on this terrible trip. I could feel my eyes well up and turned away from the bar since I didn't want Justin to see my tears.

"You, okay?" Steph pulled me close.

I felt terrible. She was the one going through a divorce, I didn't need her to support me, I was trying to support her. I shook my head and said, "Yeah, of course, I'm great." I provided probably the fakest smile I have ever smiled before. I glanced behind my shoulder and saw him there. "I just." I started to break down. "I *really* like him." I always joked, my whole life, that the minute I met an Australian man I would instantly fall in love with him. Forget love at first sight, I was planning on love at first word. I had no idea that I was just manifesting finding my perfect man. The only problem was I manifested an Australian who worked on a cruise ship knowing I would never see him again after this week. I thought back to our afternoon in his cabin. It was the first time, in a long time, that I felt *that* satisfied during a sexual experience.

Steph wrapped her arms around me. I felt warm and safe in that moment. We needed each other and it was okay that both of us were struggling. I pulled away and turned to her so we could hug each other properly. "I'm sorry your heart is feeling so broken." Her tender voice relaxed me.

"I think I could fall in love with him." I paused and felt a tear fall down my cheek, "I think I *am* falling in love." I pulled away, "How is that even possible? We've known each other for a few days." I never believed that love could happen this quickly. I always scoffed at couples that move in after a month, or movies like this where people fall instantly in love. Here I was, falling in love with someone in less than a week. I looked at Steph, "I'm sorry my brother hurt you."

Steph smiled and pulled me close. I could feel tears on my neck and her body twitching from starting to sob again.

"You will always be family, no matter what happens. And not just because of that baby." She was more emotionally my sister than Kasey ever was. Kasey was always like another mom to me, having Steph come into my life, I learned what it was like to have a close sister figure.

"Ladies." Justin's Aussie accent made me melt. "Is everything alright?"

We broke our hug and looked at Justin, tears streaming down our faces, "We're great."

Justin held out his hand and rubbed my shoulder lovingly, "How about a couple of drinks on the house?" He asked.

I nodded, "That would be amazing."

He smiled, leaned in, and gave me a quick peck on the lips. "What do you want?"

I wished he hadn't done that, "A screw-up." I glared at him as code for don't do that. His incredible eyes looking into mine melted my glare. "Like my mother always says I am." I joked.

Justin chuckled, and looked over to Steph, "And for you?"

"Just a clear soda."

Justin nodded and dashed back to the bar to get our drinks.

"You still need to be careful, what if your parents are here?" Steph looked around nervously.

"Oh please, they are the quintessential old people." I joked, "Especially after a day of hiking, they got back, had dinner at four, and were asleep by five." I guided her to a booth in a less populated corner.

"If you're sure." She didn't seem too convinced, "You never know with your parents."

I looked at her, "But the plan is to tell them everything now. Who cares?" I was hoping after calming down, she would be more on board with the idea of coming clean and having everything out in the open.

Steph was quiet.

Justin returned with two glasses on a tray, "Alright, the screw up for the far from screwed up." He placed the glass down in front of me, "And the reason my tip is cut in half" he placed the soda in front of Steph, "Your kid owes me." He joked.

Steph smiled at him, "No wonder Lori likes you so much." She grasped the straw in her glass and swished around the ice.

Justin looked at me and winked, "I like her back." He made his way back to the bar and my heart ached for him.

"This is the worst." I had never been in a situation like this before. If I wanted someone, I would usually get them. Unless they were fatphobic idiots, but once that was clear, they became a lot less attractive to me anyway. I looked at Steph who was now looking even more distraught. I realized that what I was going through was nothing compared to her, "Sorry."

She shook her head, "Pain is pain." She glanced over at the bar,

"Both of our hearts are breaking, for different reasons." She reached her hand out over the table for me to grab, so I did, "No one's pain is less valid for any reason. You know that."

My therapist had been telling me that for years, but my parents were never great at modeling that for me when I was little, so at nearly thirty, I was having to learn a lot of things that I should have known when I was a kid. My mother would always tell me on bad days that there were some kids that were homeless so I should be thankful I have a home. I sometimes wondered, in my teenage years, if it was more of a veiled threat than it was trying to put things into perspective.

I nodded and said, "I know, I just wanted this to be about you."

"You're right, I'm going to be fine." She glanced at the bar again, "Are you?"

I shrugged, "I haven't felt this way in years." My last boyfriend made me swear off relationships and just focus on hookups, which had served me well, until now.

I felt a tighter grip on my hand and looked at Steph who was smiling sweetly at me, "You're also going to be just fine."

I knew she was right. I had come back from a few heartbreaks in the past. The last one was the worst. We had moved in together, we constantly fought, and then I found a woman in our bed one night. I had vowed to never fall in love or even think about a serious relationship ever again. Here I was, longing for that familiar feeling of falling asleep to the same person every night again. I just knew that it would never work between me and Justin.

That's when it happened. Steph's phone started to ring. She looked at it, "It's your mom." She said nervously. She answered, "Hi." Her concerned face turned into one of terror as she never broke eye contact with me, "I'm with her now, we're on our way."

I started to think the worst. Maybe something happened to Dad or one of the kids. My heart raced at the thought that there was some sort of medical emergency.

Steph ended the call and set it on the table. "Your brother and Ryan were caught by your parents."

"How bad?" My heart was still racing.

"I guess they were kissing." Steph explained, "We gotta get over there." She stuck her phone in her purse as she slid out of the booth.

I looked over to Justin, "I need to go tell him we had to leave." I rushed over and immediately got Justin's attention, "Thanks for the drinks, but shit has hit the fan."

"Is everything alright?"

I shook my head, "My brother and Ryan got caught." It was time for all of us to come clean about the extensive lie that had become so overly complicated. My brother was outed, the divorce was having to be announced, and the fact that I brought my best friend on this trip not realizing he had romantic feelings toward my closeted brother. It was too impossible to explain, but I knew between the four of us, we had to explain everything now.

"Do you want me to come?" He threw the washcloth that hung over his shoulder on the bar and looked over to the other bartender, "Hey, I had an emergency, I gotta step away." He dashed around the other side of the bar before I could even answer.

"You don't have to," I protested.

"I'm coming." He looked me in the eyes and demanded as he wrapped his arm around me and guided me back to Steph.

The three of us rushed to Steph and Derrek's stateroom.

CHAPTER 21

RYAN

There we were, Derrek and I, holding each other. Derrek, married to a woman, and me supposedly in love with their daughter.

"Mom, Dad." I could feel Derrek tense in my arms, his heart was beating fast, I could almost feel it against my own chest, or was that *my* heart?

"What is going on?" I thought that Leslie was going to have a heart attack right there in front of us.

I looked at Derrek, somehow, we were frozen in place, holding each other. "I think it's time." I whispered. I didn't want him to be outed like this. I wanted him to have this conversation on his own terms, but there was nothing we could do about it now. I finally let go of Derrek and turned to his parents.

"Ryan, how dare you cheat on our daughter!" Leslie stormed up to me and gave me an old movie slap right across my face.

"Mom!" Derrek shouted.

She turned to him, "Don't you get me started, you're married."

"Lori and I aren't even together!" I rubbed my cheek, "It was all a lie." I moved away from Leslie in fear that she would hit me again.

"A lie? Why?" Jack walked into the room and closed the door.

I looked at Leslie, "Because *you* make her feel less than dirt because she isn't in a relationship and doesn't want kids." I blasted at her in an accusatory tone. If we were going down, we were going down in a flame of glory. "I sat here, silently, all week as you tore your daughter down, as you made her feel like crap. I had to fall asleep to her crying because of *you*. She felt like she needed to lie just to make this trip even slightly bearable for herself, and even when you thought she was engaged, it was never good enough."

Leslie glared at me, "You're not a member of this family, and now I know you never will be, you have no right to speak to me that way."

"I think I do." I retorted. "I *do* love your daughter after all. Maybe not in a romantic way, but she's my best friend, and has been my rock since we met." I stepped away since I was getting heated and didn't want to say something I was going to regret.

"But apparently, you love our son." Leslie's voice broke through her anger, "Our *straight* son."

"I'm," Derrek finally started to chime in, "I'm not straight, Mom." His voice trembled as the words that he never thought he would say finally came out. I knew that had to be the most difficult thing he had ever had to say. I know it was for me.

I walked over to him and put my hand on his shoulder for comfort.

Leslie shook her head, "No, this boy has filled your head with thoughts." Her voice was full of panic as she looked at the two of us. Her panic started to move to a glare that was directed at me and me alone.

Derrek shook his head. "No, Mom. I felt this way before I met Ryan." His voice was weak, and he couldn't make eye contact, so he just looked down at his feet. "I just never told you two because I was afraid." He finally looked up at them, "I never fully told anyone, not Lori, Kasey, Dave," he looked down again, "or Steph."

His parents just stood there looking at Derrek, in complete silence. The looks on their faces said it all. They were confused, hurt, angry, and pretty much every other emotion you can be. I knew it all too well. The coming out story was never easy. Telling your parents that they never fully knew their child was the most painful experience a child and parent could go through. It shouldn't be that way, but it is.

I wasn't sure how the rest of this was going to play out. I just knew I needed to stay quiet now. I wished I could disappear or teleport somewhere far from here. I wanted them to have this moment without the stress of a practical stranger among them.

"And you love this boy?" Leslie finally asked through tears.

Derrek and I looked at each other, "I think we could love each other." He explained, "We've been exploring."

"Son," Jack's voice was gentle and caring, "You're married."

Derrek took a deep breath, "We weren't going to announce it on this trip. Steph and I are splitting up. We decided to get divorced a few weeks ago." Tears started to fall down his face, "We wanted this trip to be a pleasant one."

"The baby?" Leslie asked.

"All three of us are excited to raise the baby together." Derrek reached for my hand and took it in his.

"I need to call Steph." Leslie turned and walked out of the stateroom.

"Oh, God." I said out loud, realizing that everything was unraveling, and Lori had no idea.

"Do you still love me?" Derrek pleaded to his father, it was heartbreaking.

Jack walked up to Derrek and pulled him into a deep loving hug, "Of course we do." The two held each other in that embrace for minutes as they both cried.

I stroked Derrek's back lovingly as we waited for the girls to learn that all of the lies were finally over.

Ten minutes later, Leslie sat on the couch in the stateroom, she had been silent since calling Steph. Derrek and I stood by the sliding glass door looking at her waiting for her to speak, and Jack sat next to his wife stroking her back with the same tenderness that I had for Derrek earlier.

Steph, Lori, and Justin piled into the room.

"Mom, I can explain," Lori immediately blurted out.

Leslie shook her head. "There's no need." She looked up at Lori with her eyes red and puffy, "Am I that awful to you that you felt like you needed to lie about your love life?"

Lori's eyes immediately began to water as she looked around trying to stop the tears, "You're not awful, Mom." She paused. "You just have very different views, and sometimes," she paused again.

I secretly rooted for her that she would finally tell her mother the whole truth.

"A lot of times, you become very hurtful and honestly, toxic for me." Seems like the money she pays for that therapist finally paid off. "You belittle everything that makes me feel alive, Mom." She sat next to her mom and wiped away a tear. "Mom, I love you and I want to keep you in my life, but yes, sometimes I feel like I have to keep the peace to just make time with you not hurt." She admitted. She then looked at me, her eyes telling me she was sorry for all of this, "This time, I felt it was safest to lie to keep the peace." Her voice was remorseful.

My heart hurt for Lori, "It's my fault." I finally said it was the first time I had spoken in nearly a half hour.

Lori looked at me and shook her head, "I should never have put you in this situation." She told me, "This is all on me. Everything." She walked up to me, "I am so sorry." She said to both me and Derrek.

"It's not all your fault." Derrek pulled her into a hug.

"It is. I should have just told the truth and come here alone." She pulled out of the hug and looked over to Justin. "It would have been easier." She walked up to him with that same apologetic look on her face.

Justin grabbed her and pulled her close as he kissed her forehead.

"So, when I saw you two." Leslie was finally starting to put everything together.

Lori turned to her mom. "We've been seeing each other this

week." I was going to leave out the incredible sex part and felt it was probably best.

Leslie looked so hurt, "I don't want my children to lie to me." She looked at Lori then turned to look at Derrek, "I also don't want my children to omit major parts of their life."

"Sorry, Mom." Both Lori and Derrek said in unison.

For the first time, I saw them as the kids that Leslie raised. My heart, also for the first time, ached for Leslie. She wasn't a monster. She handled things poorly, but she wasn't the evil villain that I had seen all week. She hurt her children in ways that I could never condone, but she was far from irredeemable.

She walked up to Lori and hugged her, then she made her way to Derrek and pulled him into a hug as well. She reached her arm out for Lori to join this other hug. Lori obliged and accepted the group hug, "I love my children."

"No one doubted that, Mom," Derrek told her.

She said nothing and just held them in her arms as she cried.

It was good that she seemed to finally understand what she had put her children through. I just hoped she understood. That she could piece together that the reason they lied was because of how she treated them. I didn't want them to abandon their mother, which should always be the last choice, but I would support them if they decided to go with no contact.

I made eye contact with Justin, and we shared a smile. We both knew that this meant that everything was going to be okay.

Later, after the dust had settled, we sat together in the stateroom, "So, Justin, tell us about yourself," Leslie asked.

Justin looked surprised, "Well, I'm from Australia and I've been working on cruise ships for years." He told everyone.

"So, how's that going to work dating our daughter?" Jack asked, concerned.

Lori jumped in, "We haven't talked about any of that."

"Well, the trip is almost over, you need to have that conversation soon." Leslie judgingly glanced at Justin.

"We just haven't had a great opportunity." Lori explained as she started to shut down again.

"Look, everyone here has a lot to figure out." I explained hoping to get Justin off the hot seat.

"I care deeply about your daughter; I just want to make that clear." Justin explained as he wrapped his arm around Lori.

Leslie started to cry again, "I just wish you both felt like you didn't have to hide important aspects of your lives."

"We know, and we're sorry for that." Derrek said to his mother.

Lori nodded with a kind look on her face. She stepped forward and placed her hand on her mother's shoulder, "We'll work on keeping you in the loop, but you also need to work on judging us less when we make decisions you don't agree with."

Leslie smiled at Lori and then Derrek before pulling them both into a hug, "I really am sorry."

In that moment, I saw hope in possible reconciliation between my best friend and her mother, as long as Leslie was able to walk the walk.

The next morning, I woke up next to Derrek. We had decided before we all parted that Steph would stay with Leslie and Jack for the last two nights so Derrek and I could spend some time together. It also provided the freedom for Lori and Justin to spend time together as well.

Derrek was still asleep, so I just looked at him. Yesterday, he said that we *could* love each other, what he didn't know was that I already did love him. I hadn't told him yet, but I was already deeply in love, and I wanted to tell him. I leaned over and kissed his forehead as he started to stir awake.

"Morning," I said with a smile.

He smiled back, "Morning."

Now was the perfect time. I took a deep breath and said, "I love you." My heart sank as I said it hoping he would say it back, but I knew that his heart was still a little conflicted.

"I love you too." He said as he scooted closer to me, and we kissed.

I wanted to stay like this forever. Derrek and I in paradise, in bed, kissing. This was good. This was what every decision I made in life was leading me to. A life with Derrek. I pulled him closer, and we tangled ourselves together as we lay together for what felt like hours.

CHAPTER 22

LORI

The night before was one of the most emotional I had had in a while. Justin had managed to stay with me overnight by telling his boss that his girlfriend was on the ship and that she had had an emergency. It made me feel good to hear him call me his girlfriend.

As much as I am sure both of us wanted to make love again, we decided to just hold each other all night. It felt good. He felt good, he felt right. I still knew that anything we might have would be messy since he loved his job, and I was not about to throw all my hard work away and get a random job on a cruise ship. All I knew was I wanted to be with him, and it was clear last night that he felt the same way.

I looked at him, his shaggy blonde hair fell over his eyes. He was so cute. I reached and moved his hair and tucked it behind his ears. I smiled at the thought that he was mine. I rolled over and out of bed. I meandered over to the coffee pot and started brewing some coffee. I looked outside and saw that the sun was beginning to rise over the ocean. We had departed during our family debacle and didn't notice before going to bed. I made my way out to the balcony and just daydreamed that this was my vacation. A relaxing time with the man I loved, or at least could love, watching this beautiful sunrise.

Justin's arms wrapped around me and his lips were on my neck. I rolled my head to one side and let out a moan. "Good morning." I said through my moan.

"Good morning, my love." His voice, his accent, the way he touched me. I turned around to face him, and he kissed me. Deeply and passionately, we held each other in our arms.

My legs became weak at his touch. I figured this was still part of my daydreaming.

His hands, like the day before, started to investigate my body. He slid his hand down my panties and started to touch me.

"Oh shit." I fell forward into him.

"Come back to bed." He requested as his fingers left me and he took my hand and guided me back to the king bed. "So much better than my silly little bunk." He told me as he gently guided me down to the bed.

I removed my night shirt and tossed it to the side of the bed. The anticipation built in my body.

Justin lowered himself on top of me and kissed me more deeply than ever. His tongue tickled mine for a few moments until he decided to explore my body with his lips. He moved down to my neck.

I moaned as he gently kissed my neck and then licked his way down to my breast. I forgot what it was like. What it was like to be so turned on by someone, for sex to be more than a casual hookup, to care about the other person. Casual sex is fun in its own way, but for me, being with someone that I cared about was far better sex.

Goosebumps exploded all over my body as his tongue glided down to my breasts. He stopped at them for a bit as he sucked on my nipples starting on the left before moving to the right. They hardened at his touch.

His hand reached down and touched my clit which sent waves through my body like an electrical current. His lips worked my nipples and his hand worked my clit. I was already in heaven. After a few moments, his mouth journeyed down to between my legs. He grabbed onto my panties and slid them off. He leaned back into me and glided his tongue onto my clit.

I arched my back and let out a loud moan. I reached back and grabbed the headboard as my blood began to race through my body. "Oh, God." My heart pounded faster and faster.

Justin slid two of his fingers into my opening and rubbed my G-Spot without missing a beat of licking my clitoris.

"Shit." I chanted as my body charged up until I orgasmed with a loud, "fuck!"

He peered up at me and removed his boxers exposing his erect penis.

I reached for it and took it in my hands to give it some love. I stroked it gently. I let go and maneuvered around to place it in my mouth. I took the tip and sucked and licked while my hand worked on the shaft.

Justin reached for the box of condoms left on the nightstand and took one out of the package.

I released him from my grip and laid back, anticipating what was to come. "Fuck me," I pleaded.

He kissed me again; I could taste me all over his mouth. He guided his cock inside me.

I reached for the headboard again as he thrust into me.

He lifted my legs and rested them against his chest and shoulders as he pounded into me. He started at a slower pace and then upped the tempo every minute or so. He slid against my G-Spot in this position so easily.

My body tingled as the goosebumps multiplied all over my body. "Fuck." I felt like crying as my body neared a second orgasm. It was rare for me to have two orgasms during the same session, but here we were.

He lowered my legs to his sides and lowered himself and our lips joined together again.

I let go of the headboard and reached for his ass. I grasped his cheeks as they tensed and relaxed with every pump he delivered into my vagina.

I threw my head back as my body began to pulsate with my heart. "Oh, God!" I called out as my body convulsed and I orgasmed again. This was more intense than our last time. I kissed him again as he continued to thrust into me. I knew he was getting closer as well as he started moving faster and grunted.

"Oh fuck" He collapsed on top of me as he too orgasmed, "Fuck." He said again as he rolled off me.

"I second that." My eyes were shut as I tried to keep feeling the orgasm. I opened my eyes and looked at him, I knew I had to ask, I knew we needed to have this conversation. "What are we going to do?"

Justin looked at me, still breathing hard, sweat beading on his forehead. He shook his head, "I don't know."

I sat up; the buzz was killed. I looked at him, "I really like you." I admitted.

Justin sat up and started to kiss my neck again, "I like you too." He rested his head on my shoulder, "I'm not the kind of guy to hook up with a guest." He had mentioned that before, this time it was to prove his feelings for me.

"So, how can we make this work, you being out in the Caribbean for most of the year? What happens if you get moved back to an Australian cruise? What happens if you get moved to the Mediterranean Sea?" My brain took me down a dark road of him being moved farther and farther away and making it impossible to be together with me in California. My heart started racing and my breathing became shallow and quicker. I don't have panic attacks much anymore, but when I do, it feels like I'm dying.

Justin kissed my neck again followed by him rubbing my shoulders, "Relax, we'll figure it out." He reassured me.

"Justin, we can't. This will never work." I knew we had to face reality. His first love was cruising, no matter how much he felt for me.

"Then let's enjoy our last full day together without worrying about the future." He continued to rub my shoulders which helped my adrenaline return to normal.

"When do you start work?" I turned to face him.

He shook his head, "I am free all day." He said with a smile.

"Even after calling out the rest of the night?" I didn't want him to jeopardize anything he loved.

"My girlfriend is in crisis. Even if they tried, I would tell them no." He finally released my shoulders and laid back in bed.

There it was again. My heart skipped when he said, girlfriend. Each time he said it I reconsidered the idea of staying in California. That thought faded just as quickly as it entered my brain. "We need to meet my family for breakfast." I slipped out of bed and looked at Justin. The way he looked at me, made me feel sexy, and that was the best thing about him.

I rummaged through my things and found a full outfit and Justin let out a loud sigh as I started to get dressed. "What?"

"I prefer you naked." He winked at me.

I leaned over the bed and kissed him, "Are you planning on coming to this shit show, or are you just going to stay in bed all day?" I tossed the shirt he wore last night at him.

He sat up in bed, wrapped the white button-up around his torso, and began buttoning it up. "I wouldn't miss this for the world."

I'm sure anyone would like a front-seat ticket to explaining to my nieces and nephew that the person they were introduced to at the beginning of the week was my best friend, who happened to be gay, so *not* my fiancé but was now dating their uncle. I collapsed back on the bed. "Oh, my God." I had become delirious at this point. I had caused so much drama on this trip, "What is wrong with me?"

Justin stroked my back, "Nothing is wrong with you."

I turned my head to look at him, "I lied to my family and caused all of this." I wouldn't blame my family if they all ended up hating me. I sat up facing Justin, "Had I not done what I did, no one would be miserable."

"From where I was last night, no one is miserable. Everyone has accepted this and moved on. It's just updating your sister and her family, right?" He was right, I was doing what I always do. If I thought about it long enough, I would be able to figure out how it was my fault that people couldn't breathe underwater and make a public apology to the world.

"Will you be there?" I asked again, this time wanting him to come and support me.

He nodded, "I already told you I wouldn't miss this for anything."

Justin and I headed down to where we were meeting everyone for breakfast. He was still wearing his bartender uniform from last night.

I looked at him as we entered the elevator and pressed for the promenade deck, "Not exactly how I wanted to introduce my ..." I paused, "boyfriend to my family." I joked as I straightened out his shirt. I ran my hands down his abs, I was tempted to jump him right there in the elevator.

Justin leaned down and kissed me, "I think this is perfect." He took my hand and spun me around like we were dancing, "Considering the web of lies you spun, I think this is exactly perfect." He joked.

"That's not funny." I tried to hold in a laugh.

He nodded his head, "Oh, it's hilarious." He pulled me in for another kiss as the elevator informed us that we had made it to our floor and the doors opened.

I felt the anxiety rise again. This was it; all my lies were coming to a head. Justin wrapped his hand around mine, interlacing our fingers. I rested my head on his shoulder as we walked to the café where we were meeting my family. "You know, it's been a long time since I introduced a boyfriend to my family." It was easier to say the second time. "I just wish this wasn't so complicated." I worried that how complicated I had made everything with our relationship would scare him off, "I promise I'm not this much of a drama queen normally."

He kissed the top of my head, "If this is the worst I deal with, we're good."

I wrapped myself around his arm and squeezed tightly as we walked together, "It's been a while since I've felt like this." I admitted to him.

He rested his head on mine and said, "I am not sure I ever felt this way."

I started to think, if that was true, was there a chance that I was worth walking away from his cruise life? I would never ask that of him, but what if he did? What if he feels fulfilled and wants to start a life with me in California? I squeezed him tighter as we entered the café. I immediately saw the back of Kasey's head and her family, "Here we go." I let go of Justin and sat down with them.

Justin sat next to me and awkwardly smiled at the others. "Hi, everyone."

Steph was the next one to arrive, only minutes after Justin and I did. She sat at the table across from me. She made eye contact with everyone with a closed-mouth smile and no words.

"Where's Uncle Derrek?" Grant asked.

"Not sure, I slept in your grandparents' room last night." Steph advised. She looked at Kasey, then Dave, then me. She noticed Justin, "Justin."

"Steph."

You could cut the tension in the room with a knife. I leaned over to Justin and whispered, "I thought everything was okay."

"I thought so too." He responded.

I saw Ryan and Derrek approach the table together and they sat down. Derrek was next to Justin and Ryan was next to Derrek. Here it was, just my parents then I had to come clean.

"How'd you sleep?" Derrek asked Steph.

She shrugged, "I slept fine."

"What's going on?" Lilly asked.

It was then that my parents arrived and sat with us. "That's why we wanted to get everyone together." My mother said sternly. She looked over to me, "Lori." She winked to let me know that she wasn't angry with me.

I nodded, "Okay, so, Ryan isn't my fiancé." I made eye contact with my best friend apologetically. "He's my best friend, and we *do* live together, but I lied." That anxiety was rising again.

"So, is he your boyfriend?" Becky didn't look up from her coloring page in front of her.

I shook my head, "No, Ryan only likes to date boys." I explained.

Becky dropped her crayon and looked at me, "He dates *boys*? That's weird."

Kasey patted Becky on the back, "Sweetheart, that's not weird. Sometimes, boys like to date boys, and some girls like to date girls. There are also some people who don't care if you're a boy or a girl."

Becky gazed at her mom and nodded, still confused but accepting of the new information.

I then looked to Justin, "Justin, who you all met yesterday, he and I have been seeing each other on the ship."

"So, he's your boyfriend?" Becky was confused.

I wasn't sure how to answer that question, we had used the term between each other, but mostly in jest or a way to get him out of work last night.

Justin put his arm around my chair and answered, "Yes."

My heart started fluttering, he just told my family he was my boyfriend, I looked back to Becky then to the rest of my family, "Yes, Justin is my boyfriend."

Justin and I smiled at each other, and he pulled me closer.

"So, is that it?" Grant asked as if this was the stupidest reason, we called a family meeting.

"Is everyone ready?" a female server approached the table with a pad of paper ready in hand.

"We're just gonna do the buffet." My dad advised her.

"Sounds great, it's in the back room and all you can eat. I'll be back with your check later." She said with a smile as she walked away from our table.

"No, that isn't it." I said sheepishly as I glanced over to Derrek.

Derrek nodded at me, "Your Aunt Steph and I decided we don't want to be married anymore." He looked over to Steph kindly, "It wasn't a decision that we took lightly, and it was made a few weeks before our trip."

Lilly looked at Steph, "You're not gonna be our aunt anymore?" She seemed so sad. Lilly and Steph always had a special relationship.

"Steph will always be family." I reached my hand out over the table reaching for my niece.

"That's right, Steph is always going to be part of this family." My mother reiterated. "Especially when your new little cousin comes around."

Steph nodded, "This is a difficult decision that we've come to, but your Uncle Derrek deserves to be happy."

"So, Aunt Steph stopped making you happy?" Lilly asked, "Do you not love each other anymore?"

Derrek shook his head, "I love your Aunt Steph very much, and that will never change. She deserves to be happy too." He took a pause to look over at Steph before continuing, "Being a grown-up can be complicated, and your Aunt Steph and I just feel like it's best to move on and date other people." He then sat back in his chair and took a deep breath, "Which leads me to the next announcement. On this trip, I decided I wanted to date Ryan."

Becky looked at Derrek with shock and yelled loud enough for the entire café to hear, "You date *boys* too?"

Derrek's eyes widened and everyone else laughed. It was a great mood boost at the table. Derrek then said, "Yes."

"So, that's why you don't want to be with Aunt Steph anymore? You don't wanna date girls?" Becky asked so naively

Derrek shook his head, "I don't think I care if someone is a boy or a girl. I just like people."

Kasey smiled at our younger brother, leaned over to her youngest child, and said, "Sometimes, people just love people."

"It's weird." Becky said again.

Kasey shook her head, "It's not weird, love is always a good thing."

Lilly looked at her little sister then over to Derrek, "Do you love Ryan?"

Derrek thought for a moment, then answered, "I do. I think I have for a long time. Before I realized that I wanted to date him." He grabbed Ryan's hand and Ryan smiled.

"So, if you love Aunt Steph and Ryan, then why don't you just date both of them?" Lilly asked.

"Some people do that. I'm not sure Aunt Steph wants it that way." Derrek answered.

"So, is that all? Or can we finally eat?" Grant seemed unphased by the information that he was presented with.

"That's all the lies I either told or kept." I explained then said, "I'm sorry that I lied."

Becky looked at me earnestly and said, "I think Grandma should ground you."

My mom laughed and said, "That's it, Lori, you're grounded, starting when you get back to California."

I nodded, "A much-deserved punishment."

CHAPTER 23

RYAN

After breakfast and the dust had finally been cleared, we all headed back to the rooms with our clothes to get changed into swimsuits. We were at sea all day and planned on spending the whole day as a family. Adults would be day drinking and the kids would be swimming. For the first time, I felt like I belonged to the family.

"How does it feel?" Lori asked as she clasped her bikini behind her back. "To have Derrek finally be out?"

"It feels good." I grabbed my trunks out of the drawer I used for the week. "I was worried that I was gonna be in another relationship where my boyfriend wasn't going to tell his family." I knew I couldn't handle a relationship like that.

"I'm just glad we aren't engaged anymore." Lori joked as she grabbed a book and her sunglasses.

"So, what's Justin's plan?" I hoped she would get one more day with him before they would be separated and eventually stop talking. Which broke my heart for her.

"He has the day off and he will be joining us." She was so giddy. It had been a couple of years since I had seen her fall in love.

"Have you ever fallen in love this fast?" I asked her.

She shook her head, "I am not in love."

"Yes, you are." I smirked as I opened the door after a knock, revealing Justin, "And there he is now."

"Hey," Justin said as he walked in the door.

"Hey!" Lori looked around, "I am ready."

The three of us walked to Derrek and Steph's room. They were waiting for us at the door. I was met with a wave by Derrek.

"Alright, looks like we're all ready, this very weird family we have going on." Steph seemed to be in a better mood since yesterday.

We made our way to the pool and saw our family that had saved enough lounge chairs for all the adults.

"Over here!" Leslie called out as she waved frantically.

Our group approached and each placed towels on a lounge chair. Steph parked on the other side of Justin who was next to Lori. I was next to Lori on the other side and Derrek was next to me.

"Uncle Derrek, come swimming with me!" Becky called from the steps going into the pool.

I saw him smile over to her and then look at me.

"Go, you've been commanded." I joked.

Derrek nodded took off his shirt and headed toward the pool. It was fun to watch him swim with her, it was clear she hadn't fully learned how to swim on her own yet. He held her by her hands and guided her as she frantically kicked her legs and spit water out every few seconds. "You got this!" He called out laughing.

I felt a nudge on my shoulder, "You ready for all of that?" Lori asked.

I was. I wanted a family more than anything. I knew Lori didn't seem to have a desire, but I sure did. I wanted kids, I wanted kids with Derrek. I nodded, "I still can't believe you don't."

She looked at her brother, "I like that." She pointed. "I like the fun parts. I like being an aunt. I can play and have fun, but I don't have to do the tough part. I don't have to worry about raising good humans. I don't have to deal with sleepless nights. I still have freedoms that parents just don't have."

I nodded, "I can understand that." I wrapped my arm around her, "I can't believe that one day, you'll be my kids' actual aunt instead of that close friend close enough to be one." It warmed my heart to know that with the way things looked at this point, we were going to *be* family.

Lori nuzzled into me, "I can't wait."

Kasey walked up to the two of us, "Let's go."

"Where?" Lori asked.

"Over to the bar, I am buying everyone a drink and we are toasting this crazy family vacation and the two knew hostages." She joked. "Derrek, enough swimming lessons, the adults are going to drink!"

"Okay!" Derrek pulled Becky back to the stairs and she ran off to the kiddy pool where she seemed to quickly meet a new friend and they immediately started playing.

I followed the group, even Steph, to the bar. Derrek and I sat at the bar next to Justin and Lori.

Lori ordered a Vodka Sprite, Justin a Gin and Tonic, Derrek a Margarita, and I ordered a Pina Colada.

Kasey raised her vodka cranberry and said, "To Justin and Ryan, may they understand that we are only slightly crazy and not get too scared off."

We all clinked our glasses and took a drink.

I smiled at Derrek and then over to Lori and Justin who seemed to be making up for the lost time of sneaking around most of the trip.

I wrapped my free hand around Derrek, "I can't believe we're heading home tomorrow." The ship was docking nice and early in the morning and we were to depart and head straight to the airport.

"Why don't you see if you can change your flight and come back to Minnesota for a little while." Derrek begged me.

I wanted to, but I also didn't want to get his hopes up. So, I simply told him, "I'll see." I knew it was not what he wanted to hear, but I also wanted to make sure that if I couldn't it wouldn't disappoint him too much.

Derrek's smile drooped and his eyes darkened. "Sure." He

turned away from me to face Lori, "Hey sis, so you two figure this whole thing out?"

"Not yet, no." Lori rolled her eyes.

"Hey." I pulled Derrek back around, "It's not that I don't *want* to, you know that right?" I didn't want to hurt his feelings, and I was afraid I had.

Derrek nodded, "Sure, of course. It's just, I thought you'd have been more excited about at least trying."

"What's going on?" Lori asked as Justin wrapped his fit arms around her waist and rested his head on her shoulder.

"Nothing, just," Derrek put his drink down and said, "I just wanna get back in the water." He walked over to the pool and slipped into the salty pool water.

Lori looked at me with a puzzled look, "What?"

"He wants me to take a detour and go to Minnesota for a little while." I explained.

"And you don't want to?" Justin started to butt into the conversation.

I shook my head, "I *do* want to. I think it would be crucial for our relationship, but ..."

"But what?" Lori asked.

"The show is starting again soon." I admitted. I didn't want to leave Lori high and dry for all the pre-production that would be starting up again soon.

"Oh please." She blasted back at me, "That won't start for like another month."

The truth was, I was afraid I wasn't going to want to leave if I went. I would want to stay with Derrek forever. "What if I stay longer?"

"Then you stay longer, it's going to be okay." Lori slapped my arm.

"Ow, why?" I laughed.

"You *need* to spend time with him, go." She demanded. "As your boss, I am laying you off until you've spent enough time in Minnesota with my brother." Her stare was aggressive, but her smile let me know that she wasn't angry.

"Yes ma'am," I saluted her and headed over to the pool. I removed my tropical button-up as I approached where Derrek seemed to be having a breath-holding contest by himself. "You know, it's a lot more fun if you have competition."

Derrek wiped the water from around his eyes and looked at me without a word. I was trying to avoid disappointing him but turns out that's exactly what I did.

"I didn't realize how important it already was to you that I try to change my flight and go home with you." I slid into the pool and looked at him. "I'm sorry. I love you and I want to go to Minnesota. I just wasn't sure how plausible it was, and I didn't want to get either of our hopes up." I explained.

Derrek remained silent then looked away trying to hold in an emotion.

"I would love to go and spend that time with you." I took his hands and held them, "I will do what I can to change my plans."

"You will?" He finally spoke to me again.

I nodded.

Derrek smiled and pulled me in for a kiss.

I could hear Kasey and Lori in the background cheering on our kiss like they were a couple of high schoolers. I did what I could not to laugh, but the laugh came out anyway as did a laugh from Derrek.

Later, we all sat around the pool with snacks and empty plates that at one point contained our lunches.

I was stuffed, "I don't think I will ever eat again." I joked as I held my stomach. It ached. It was so full. I loved eating, but this had been too much.

"Same." Derrek, on the lounge next to me, reached his hand out for mine.

I took his hand in mine as I noticed Steph come and sit on the lounge next to Derrek. I wanted to get up and leave, I wanted to give the two of them space as their relationship was coming to an end. I started to get up from the chair.

"No, stay." Steph told me.

I relaxed back down and looked over to her.

She smiled at both of us and placed her hand on her stomach, "What's important is that this baby is going to have three parents who care deeply for him." She started, "So, I need to learn how to be okay with all of this."

"Anything you need, Steph, you know that." She and I had been friends for years at this point. I would do anything for her. My feelings for her soon-to-be ex-husband didn't change my feelings for her in any way.

"Let's do something tonight, the three of us." Derrek offered.

Steph nodded. She looked at the pool, "For now, do you two just want to get in the pool? It's so hot."

I looked at Derrek and nodded at him. We all slipped into the pool and waded to the deep end.

Steph glared at me, this time it was playful, I had no idea what she was planning on doing, but I knew it was going to be something. She slipped under the water, and I could hear the Jaws theme song in my head.

I looked around hoping to see her, then I felt her hands around my ankles as she pulled them from under me and I fell under the water.

We both came up from under the water, I coughed and laughed, "What the hell, Steph?" I splashed some water at her playfully which evolved into the three of us having a water fight. For the first time, I felt as though the three of us were going to be okay and we would be star co-parents. Or this was just a moment where Steph felt like she could handle it and she would go back to hurt later. I was going to soak up this good moment as long as I could, and I knew Derrek felt the same way.

After our childish swim, the three of us headed back to our staterooms to get dressed so we could walk around the ship and get some movement in on our day.

We walked the promenade together, Derrek felt comfortable enough to hold my hand as we walked.

Steph noticed and just wrapped her arm around Derrek's free

arm and rested her head on his shoulder. "I'm sorry I've been such a terror on this trip."

Derrek kissed her head and said, "It's okay." He let go of my hand to embrace Steph, "I'm sorry things turned out the way they did."

I felt bad about all of this too. I was glad that Derrek and I finally were able to explore our feelings for each other, but if I could take away Steph's pain of watching her husband fall in love with someone else.

Steph looked at me, "I'm sorry to you too. I've treated you like some villain, and you're not."

I moved to the other side of Derrek and held out my arms for a hug, which was accepted. I pulled her into a loving embrace, "I love you so much, nothing about that will change and it kills me that I hurt you."

Steph shook her head, "You should *never* be sorry for falling in love." She squeezed me harder.

Derrek wrapped his arms around both of us and we stood there in a group hug for minutes as we put all of this pain behind us.

"What's important is that baby." I told the two of them.

I let go and through the emotion, I said, "Let's go get a drink or something." I looked at Steph, "Well, we can get you a virgin pina colada."

We made our way to a bar for that drink.

We sat in a Caribbean-themed bar, it was bright and colorful. Jamaican music played in the background. We chose a high-top table in a corner and ordered fruity drinks each, non-alcoholic for Steph.

"So, I suppose we should figure out how the three of us can successfully be in the same area." Steph played with the straw in her drink.

"Well, Ryan is in California, and he's set." Derrek told her hinting at them moving out to California.

"But we're also set in our careers in Minnesota." Steph argued.

I knew it wasn't fair to ask them both to move to California.

However, I didn't want to throw away my career and leave Lori. "There are a lot of options."

"I just don't know what options we would have in Los Angeles." Steph continued to play with her straw, this time she moved it in and out of her glass.

"There are a ton of options in LA, gotta be more than the Twin Cities." I told her, hoping she would at least consider coming out to LA and do some looking.

"But the cost of living in California is awful." She brought up a good point. Los Angeles was one of the most expensive places to live in the country.

"What if," Derrek paused. He took a deep breath and then finally said, "What if we got a place all together?"

I stayed silent; I wasn't sure what Steph would think about that idea. Derrek and I share one room, and she and the baby share another or something. It seemed like a weird sitcom waiting to happen.

"That won't happen." Steph immediately shot down that idea, "You two deserve privacy, and so do I."

"Look, I'm going to work on coming back to Minnesota after this trip for a while. We have time to figure all of this out." I told them both.

"But it's not fair for you to have to give up everything you've worked so hard for." Derrek said.

"We would be giving up our careers too." Steph argued.

"He's an animator. He has to be in specific places." Derrek told Steph. "We can get jobs just like we have in Los Angeles, Ryan would have to start with a whole new career."

Steph stopped playing with her straw and sat back, "You're right."

"I don't want to be a cause of stress." I told them.

"But you're part of this decision." Derrek told me.

I didn't want to be part of this decision, I wanted it to just be easy. I didn't want to be the reason for pain, and I already was, and it stressed me out. I was more willing to just drop my career and figure something else out and move to Minnesota.

"It's just not fair to ask that of Ryan." Derrek told Steph.

"It's also not fair for two people to pick up and move to a place that's practically unaffordable." Steph continued to argue.

I was starting to think that none of this was going to work out. I just needed to tell them that I would move to Minnesota. I wanted this argument to end. "Like I said, I'm coming out to Minnesota, maybe after that, the two of you can come out to Los Angeles. That way we can come to a decision together after we've all experienced life in both cities." I offered. I knew we weren't going to decide on the ship. There was no telling what would even happen after we all got off the ship. It's easy to fall in love in paradise. We needed to go back to our normal lives and live life together working and commuting.

Steph nodded, "I think that's the best compromise for now." She smiled at me. "How do we want to work out sleeping tonight?"

"Yeah, it's not fair to push you to Leslie and Jack's room." I thought to myself for a moment hoping to come up with something.

I was no longer comfortable with them sleeping in the same bed. So, I knew I wanted them to sleep separately. "What about you staying with Lori?" I offered it to Steph.

"I think she's going to want to be with Justin, it's their last night for who knows how long." Steph reminded me.

I nodded, "I suppose there's no good way for her to sleep in Justin's room."

"I've looked up crew cabins before because I was curious, they are basically sardine cans." Derrek explained.

"I guess my only options are Leslie and Jack or somehow squeeze into Kasey and Dave's room." Steph said.

"No, that's not fair either." I told her.

"But it's the only option that makes sense." Steph told me, "Honestly, it's fine." She finished her drink and said, "I think I'll head to my room and pack up."

"Steph, are you sure?" Derrek held out for her hand lovingly. He still loved her, and he probably always would.

Steph took his hand and smiled, "Yes, I'm sure. You two deserve time together." She smiled.

After our drinks, we all headed to the rooms we started in.

I grabbed my suitcase and opened the drawer I had been using and started packing my clothes in my luggage. Once I was totally packed up, I placed my room key on the table with a note letting Lori know that I was spending our last night with Derrek, which I knew she would understand.

I made my way to the stateroom that I would be sharing with Derrek for another night. I was giddy to move in with him. I was in love, and I couldn't wait to express that love again with him. I knocked on the stateroom door and Derrek stood there, smiling at me.

"Steph already left." He told me as he handed me her room key. "She packed up pretty fast and headed to my parent's room." He seemed slightly sad, but also relieved. All of this was coming to an end.

I smiled and stepped inside the room as I grabbed the card key and placed my luggage on the couch in the room. It was basically identical to the room I shared with Lori, just backward. One king-size bed with just enough room to move around. A great view of the ocean on the balcony. I felt Derrek's hands on my shoulders. It felt incredible to have him touch me. I turned around to face him and we kissed.

Derrek rested his hands on my chest as we kissed. I pushed him until he fell onto the bed with me. Derrek's hand wandered under my shorts. I felt him grasp me and begin to stroke.

I ended our kiss and threw my head back as I felt pleasure pulse through my cock and up through the rest of my body. I reached for him as well so we could stroke each other at the same time.

After a little simultaneous stroking, I let go and pulled away from him as I undressed myself.

Derrek smiled and also undressed, exposing his cock to me. I was hungry for him. I needed him.

I placed my mouth around his dick.

Derrek moaned with pleasure as he ran his fingers through my short curly hair. "Shit. Oh, God."

I continued to pleasure him until my mouth was filled with his juices.

Derrek stumbled and moaned, "Oh fuck that's good!"

I swallowed and crawled up his body, "I love you." I made eye contact with him, it was the first time in a long time that I said that to a man. I had never felt this deeply for someone before.

"I love you too." He was out of breath and starting to sweat.

"I want to fuck you." I smoothed his hair.

Derrek smiled and nodded as he wriggled under me flipping to his stomach, "I want that too."

I grabbed the cheeks of his fine ass and rubbed my shaft through the crack between his cheeks as I felt myself get harder. I wanted to just dive into him, but I wanted to make this our best experience. He had already orgasmed once, and I couldn't wait to give him more pleasure. My hands moved to rub up and down his back.

Derrek jiggled his ass a little pleading for me to enter him. I was going to tease him a little longer.

I laid down on top of him, my mouth right next to his ear and I whispered, "Beg me."

"Ryan, you're an ass." He half-joked.

"No, you want me in your ass." I reminded him. I liked playing this role during sex sometimes. I wanted to show him this dirty side of me, I wanted to see if this was a turn-on for him.

"Ryan!" He called out.

I could feel him tense under me, "Beg for it." I licked his ear.

"Please fuck me."

I sat back up. I stood and grabbed the condom box I swiped from the room I shared with Lori. I slipped a condom on followed by the aloe vera for lube. I slipped into him. My thrusting started timidly at first watching every micromovement on his face. His face never once showed pain, so I pumped at my normal tempo.

With every movement, Derrek's face clenched up but he continued to reassure me that everything was good. "Fuck yeah." followed by, "That feels great." Eventually, the words disappeared as it was just moans with a few "Fucks" and "Shits" when he could make words.

I grunted, matching his moans. I peered down to his face which looked to be in slight pain, "You okay?"

He nodded and continued to moan. "Fuck!" He called out. "Keep doing it just like that."

With every movement of my hips, my body warmed as I neared climax. "Oh, God!" I called out as I felt myself reaching the edge.

"Fuck, Ryan! Oh, my God!" Derrek called out as he tensed then released as he orgasmed.

I thrust a few more times into him and I too finished as I fell on top of him.

"Holy shit." Derrek said out of breath again. He reached back trying to touch me.

I grabbed his hand and rolled off him. We held hands. I could still feel my heart beating strong. I turned my head to look at him.

He was already looking at me. The loving look he gave me made me melt. "I want you to stay with me. Don't go back to California."

It was clear Derrek was scared that Steph would never agree to move to California, and he couldn't move away from the baby.

I rolled to my side and ran my fingers through his hair as I scooted closer, "Don't worry, we will be together." I promised him and intended to keep that promise.

CHAPTER 24
LORI

Justin and I settled into my stateroom for the night. He walked up behind me, moved my hair, and started to kiss my neck. It felt good. I wanted him, but I also wanted to prove that I could sleep with him without sleeping with him. I wanted to prove that we had something aside from the excitement of falling for someone that I wouldn't see again, possibly ever. I turned to face him and wrapped my arms around his neck. "I really could love you." I told him.

"Funny, because I *do* love you." He cocked his eyebrow.

I kept myself and my heart very guarded. I wanted to open it to him, but I also knew that I couldn't since I didn't know what our future looked like. I was also afraid to ask him what he saw our future as. I kissed him.

Justin moved his hands around me and unclasped my bra as he pushed his tongue into my mouth. It was clear he wanted sex. His lips moved back to my neck.

"Should we have sex?" I asked him.

"I thought you'd never ask." He said to me as he moved his hands up my shirt and started to caress my breasts.

"No, I mean, should we depend on our sexual attraction?" I felt my body melting into him.

"Yes, yes we should." He said desperately as he moved his hand under my pants and pushed a finger inside me.

I leaned against him, my head resting on his shoulder, "Oh God." I gave in to my desire and kissed him again. I figured, what's wrong with leaning on the sex if it was this good and we might not have it again.

I grabbed his shirt and pulled it off of him as he pulled my shirt off of me. I wriggled out of my bra and backed away from him. I gave him a seductive look as I sat on the edge of the bed, "Let's go then."

"God you're good." He said as he lunged at me and we fell back on the bed. He removed my shorts. I raised my hips as he dug his face into me. I felt him lick me as his hands scaled up my body to grab my breasts. He played with my nipples as he continued to play with my clit with his talented tongue.

My vagina throbbed, matching my heartbeat. "Get up here!" I commanded.

Justin obliged me and moved up to face me. We kissed again. He teased me with his cock as he moved it around my opening and rubbed it against my clit.

Now not only did I want it, I *needed* it. "Fuck me."

Justin looked around, "Where are the condoms?"

I opened my eyes and looked at him, "Oh shit, Ryan took them with him."

"Why would two men need condoms?" Justin asked.

I didn't want to talk about Ryan and my brother having sex, "Not sexy."

"Sorry, but we can't have sex without a condom." He plopped down next to me on the bed. "Damn."

"I mean, I know I'm clean, and I have an IUD." I was hoping there was still a chance for me to get off tonight.

Justin ran his finger against the small of my back, "I don't have enough sex to worry about being clean."

That surprised me, considering how good he was at it. "Then why can't we?" I crawled up next to him on the bed. His hot breath washed over my face as our noses touched.

"I just want to be responsible." He kissed me.

"Well, we can still have fun." I smiled as I slid down to his still-erect cock and took him into my mouth. I didn't love giving blow jobs all the way to orgasm, cum tasted awful and I had one boyfriend upset with me for making a face after.

"Oh, God." Justin rolled his head back.

I wrapped my hand around the shaft of his penis and sucked on the head. I glided my hand up and down.

"Oh fuck." He called out as he grabbed my hair. His fingers tangled with each strand and he tugged.

I moved my mouth a little farther down his shaft and back up. I knew how far I could go without gagging. I ran my hands up and down his thighs a few times before grabbing his ass and squeezing.

"Shit, that's good Lori." Justin placed his face in his hands.

My mouth was filled with his cum. I knew it wasn't sexy to run to the bathroom to spit it out, so I swallowed the salty cream in my mouth and cuddled back into him.

"Your turn." He said as he then slid down and placed his face between my legs.

My body trembled with anticipation as he placed his mouth on me. His tongue worked my clit and he slid two fingers inside, and he applied pressure, and stroked my G-Spot. First, it was two, then he slid a third. "Oh, God." I bit my bottom lip. I reached for his head and tugged on his blonde locks. It didn't take long for me to feel the orgasm pulse through my entire being.

He crawled back up to meet my face and kissed me. He had a proud look on his face as he ran his middle finger up and down my arm.

It tickled a little. I smiled.

"What?" He asked.

"I've never had a man give me as much pleasure as you have." I admitted. "You're just amazing at it."

"Or, maybe we just fit together." He kissed the tip of my nose gently.

We drifted off to sleep in each other's arms. I knew what

tomorrow was going to bring. Tomorrow was the day my heart was going to break.

The next morning, I woke up, slipped into my silk robe, and walked out onto the balcony to look at the port. We landed about an hour before I woke up and I felt a tear form. I looked back at Justin, that's when it hit me.

He woke up as I looked at him, "Good morning, beautiful."

"We're home." I told him. "I have to pack and leave."

Justin rose to look at me, "I know."

"I love you." I told him as tears started falling from my eyes. I rushed back to the bed and fell into his arms, "I *do* love you. I don't want to leave."

"I don't want you to go either, and I love you too." He felt so warm and comfortable. He was safe.

I wanted to stay in this moment forever. I wanted to stay, but I knew I couldn't. I knew I had to go home.

We made coffee and decided to just order room service for breakfast. We sat out on the balcony as I munched on my avocado toast, and he ate his fried eggs with toast.

My heart was full, I finally told someone I loved him. I hadn't used that word in a romantic tone for a few years, and it felt good to love again.

"So, what do we do?" I asked.

"I have another few months on the ship before I get a break." He explained, "Whenever I'm off, I go home to Australia."

Of course, he did, he is also away from his family and friends, "Well, when is that? I can make a trip to Australia work."

"You would?" He took a bite from his yolk-soaked toast with a hint of surprise across his face, "Wouldn't your show be back up and running?" He took a sip of the orange juice he had ordered. "I figure it would be hard to take time off to travel to another country."

"I'm the boss of the show, I can do what I want." I said as I took another bite. I was determined to make this work.

"Still, at best, we would see each other about two times a year, that doesn't build a good relationship. It would be easiest if you came to work on the ship." He seemed hopeful.

I shook my head, "I love you, but I don't want to uproot my life and live and work on a cruise ship." I wasn't sure I wanted to say the next thing I was about to say because I didn't know how he would react to knowing I make a lot of money, "I would end up taking a major pay cut, and I have a mortgage to worry about."

Disappointment flooded Justin's face, "Yeah."

My stateroom phone rang, I stood and went to answer it, "Hello?"

"Are you almost ready to leave the ship?" It was my mother, checking in on me as always.

"Just having a quiet breakfast with Justin." I told her, realizing that we were never going to make this work. I hung up with my mother and joined him back out on the balcony, "I guess we're getting ready to depart."

Justin nodded as he had finished his food, "I'll walk you out."

I packed as quickly as I could and looked at the bed I was able to share with Justin for a couple of nights.

He kissed my cheek from behind and said, "We will figure this out." It was nice to hear him be hopeful, but I was convinced that everything was ending at that moment.

We made our way to where my family planned on meeting to leave the ship together, I saw my family, and we approached.

"There they are!" My mother called out with a smile. She moved past me and pulled Justin in for a hug, "It was wonderful to meet you."

"It was amazing to get to know all of you." Justin smiled at my whole family before turning to me. "You," he said with love in his eyes, "I am going to miss the hell out of you." He moved my hair behind my ears, "October, Australia." He told me as he handed me a piece of paper.

I took it and looked at it. It was his number for his cell phone, his number out in Australia, and the address of his place in Melbourne. I looked at him as tears started to form in my eyes again, I nodded, "Thank you." I quickly pulled out a notebook I had and made sure he had my number too. We shared one more kiss before he disappeared into the crowd to return to his life as a bartender on the ship.

My mother placed her hand on my shoulder, "Are you okay?" She asked.

I turned to her and shook my head no.

She pulled me into a hug as I sobbed in her arms, "You're going to be okay, baby."

I felt my heart breaking knowing that the trip to Australia would never happen. I would probably never hear from him again and I was devastated.

"If he loves you, like wholly loves you, you will see him again, and he will take steps to be with you. This ship cannot be more important than his love for you." She pushed me out of the hug to look into my eyes, "And if this ship is his first love, then you don't need him."

I nodded. "Thanks, Mom."

My heart completed its shattering as I walked down the ramp and off the ship. I turned to face the ship one last time and up on the deck, I saw Justin looking down at me.

He waved.

CHAPTER 25
RYAN

We made our way to the airport. Last night, I stayed up late to work on changing my flight to Minneapolis instead of Los Angeles. I looked at Lori as she sat alone. I knew all that was on her mind right now was her last image of Justin on the deck of the ship. Now, I had to tell her that I was leaving her alone in her heartbreak and that killed me.

I sat next to her, "Would you hate me if I told you that I changed my flight to Minneapolis to start working on this mess with Derrek and Steph?"

Lori looked at me with a forced smile, "You idiot, no, I wouldn't hate you. I would judge you if you didn't." She hugged me, "You *can* be with the man you love, be with him."

"But you're hurting." I squeezed her harder. I wanted to take away all the pain in her heart, even though I knew I couldn't.

"And you're a phone call away." She told me, "I will be okay."

I wanted to believe that, but I knew that she would just eat her feelings and watch romcoms the whole time I would be away from her. "Are you sure?"

"Even if it wasn't, it's too late to change it back." She put her hands on my cheeks, "You go and be with the man you love."

I smiled and pulled out of her grasp and then gave her a peck on the lips, "I gotta say, I had a lot of fun in my first engagement."

Lori smiled, more genuinely now, "I'm glad I could be your first fiancé."

"Thank you for turning my world upside down." Had she not come up with this crazy lie, things with Derrek might never have progressed. I owed her for this weird, tangled web. Even if it got us in deep water for a little while.

"Go." She said as she looked past me looking at her brother.

"I love you." I told her.

"I love you too, more than you will ever know." She said, "I will be just fine."

I gave her another kiss and joined Derrek's family as we headed to the gate to Minneapolis, which was pretty far from Lori's gate.

"She's incredibly resilient, she'll be okay." Leslie told me as she noticed my look back to her still sitting alone at her gate.

We reached our gate and I saw Kasey approach me. She wrapped her arm around my shoulder, "How about that drink." She looked at Steph, "Can you watch the kids?"

Steph rolled her eyes and nodded, "Sure, I got it."

"Great, I just need to get to know my brother's new boyfriend." She said with a sly smile at me.

I was a little embarrassed to hear that term, but it also felt wonderful, "You got to know me all week."

"As my sister's fiancé!" She argued.

"That *was* me, just not being totally honest about my sexual orientation, or which family member I was into." I realized how crazy that sounded coming out of my mouth.

"Nope, to me, you're a whole new person. Buy me a drink." Kasey grabbed me and dragged me off. She liked me a lot better as Derrek's boyfriend than she did as Lori's fiancé.

Later, we all boarded the plane back to Minneapolis. "So, how far is Burnsville from the airport?" I plopped down in my window seat.

"Not long at all." Derrek stuffed his large carry-on into the overhead compartment, "Maybe a fifteen-minute drive."

"Depending on snow." Steph answered disappointed.

I was glad to have found a seat on this flight on such short notice, this wasn't exactly prime travel time for Minnesotans, I guess. I was worried that I was going to end up on a different flight which would have been very lonely. I wanted to spend every moment with Derrek right now.

Derrek slid into his seat next to me and leaned into cuddle, "Thanks for coming back to Minnesota with me."

"So, what do you want to show me first?" I was excited to see his home through his eyes. "I've never been to Minnesota."

"Oh man, I have no idea, I guess the Mall of America?"

I nodded, "I've always wanted to at least see that place." I leaned in and kissed him.

The plane took off and we cuddled the whole way to Minnesota. After around three hours, we landed.

I glanced out the window and saw a blanket of snow on the ground around the airport. It was beautiful. I rarely see it now. "Wow."

"It's snow, it's not that exciting." Derrek leaned in and looked out the window with me. "I was hoping it would be gone by the time we got back."

"I guess I had no idea you had snow this late in the year." It was March, after all.

"The only month we haven't had some sort of snowfall is July, believe it or not." Derrek had to be kidding, but his face was serious.

"How did you survive all this time?"

Derrek laughed, "Snow isn't even the worst of it all," Derrek looked into my eyes, "The cold is what could kill you."

"Lori has complained about the negative temps to me before, it sounds awful." I wasn't in a rush to visit Minnesota after I heard those stories. "But you'll keep me warm, right?" I cuddled in close.

"Of course."

After a few more minutes, we began departing the plane, and as I stepped into the tunnel that led to the airport. I felt a burst of cool air and it became clear to me, "I don't have a coat." I was now terrified.

"It's not even that cold." Derrek pointed out.

"Anything below fifty degrees is cold." Los Angeles weather was very different from here. "I'm going to die." I was officially convinced of this.

"I'm sure they have coats at a shop here at the airport." Derrek started glancing around as we made our way into the building. We continued walking around the airport in hopes of finding a coat. "And if we have to, I can show you the Mall right away." He smiled.

"How are we gonna do that, I don't have a coat." I knew the Mall wasn't attached to the airport.

"Because the train is just downstairs, and it goes right to the Mall of America, and you'll only feel like you're outside for a few minutes getting into the Mall." He explained.

I didn't want to be outside at all, but I guess if it meant I was getting a coat, it made enough sense, "What about your car?" I asked.

"We all parked at a park-n-ride on the train line and took the train here. I thought that was a lot smarter than parking at the airport, which always costs a bundle."

Luckily, after looking for about ten minutes, we did find a place with jackets, which was better than the T-shirt I was in. "Will this be enough?" I asked as I held the windbreaker up to my chest.

"No, but it will get you by until we can get you to my apartment and you can take one of my coats." He told me.

I nodded, "Good enough." I brought it to the counter and purchased it. I nearly reached into my wallet to tip the cashier and remembered that we were back in the real people world and not on the ship anymore.

The whole family met at the train platform, "I guess I had no idea that Minnesota had a subway system."

"We don't, it's just a subway at the airport so it can go under the runway." Kasey grabbed Lilly's hand as we waited for the train.

"Interesting." I knew very little about public transportation in Minnesota.

Jack approached everyone with little slips of paper, "Here are your tickets." He handed me one.

I looked at it, "So we give this to someone when we get on?" I asked.

"Only if they ask for it." Steph answered.

"I remember one time when Grant was little, Dad and I took him downtown. It was the only time we had been asked for our tickets, but Grant panicked because he didn't have one." Derrek laughed.

"I did?" Grant had been so young, it wasn't a surprise he didn't remember.

"Yeah, so I gave you the receipt from the Light Rail tickets and told you that that was your ticket. Then you handed it to the security guy and said, 'Here's my ticket!'" Everyone laughed.

Grant looked embarrassed, "Guys." His face was very red.

"Relax, we think it was cute." Kasey playfully shoved her son.

The train stopped and we all boarded one of the cars that was headed toward the Mall of America and whatever my new life consisted of. I wasn't sure if I would end up here in Minnesota, or if the three, eventually the four, of us would go back to California.

CHAPTER 26

LORI

stepped into my condo, and I dropped my suitcase to the floor with a loud thud. I sighed and looked over my well-kept condo.

I meandered over to the floor-to-ceiling window that overlooked some mountains, leaving my travel bags at the door. The silence was deafening. Life on the ship felt so alive all the time, and I had Ryan and my family. That week changed my life forever, but I was heartbroken because of it.

I gazed over the range of mountains in front of me, I had never felt more alone. I was in love, and I had someone in love with me. I wiped away a tear that fell from my eye.

"Ugh!" I cried as I rushed to my modern kitchen to get my first drink back. I reached for the freezer and pulled out my cranberry-flavored vodka. My mixer was on top of my fridge. I added ice, poured the vodka, grabbed my triple sec, and poured that in after. I turned back to my fridge and pulled out a lime. I cut it in half and squeezed one of the halves into the mixer. I slipped the lid on and shook all my heartache out.

In the corner of my kitchen, I store my martini glasses. It felt like such a long way, but after a few of these, I wasn't going to care. I made my way to the cabinet with my mixer and poured the drink into one of my martini glasses.

I didn't even sit down before I started drinking my very alcoholic Cosmopolitan. Cranberry vodka was the best invention ever, I didn't have to water down my drink anymore with cranberry juice.

"It's way too quiet in here." I grabbed my phone and opened my music app and synced to my Bluetooth speakers. After things with my last boyfriend ended, I created a playlist of sad breakup songs, so I opened that playlist and blasted the music as I continued to drink.

After twenty songs, a second martini, and an hour of crying, the music cut out. I was caught by surprise and just as I grabbed my phone to see why, a very strange number popped up on my phone. "What is this?" My heart sank as I saw the city of Melbourne listed under the strange number. *Could it be?* I answered the phone, "Hello?"

"Hey." It was Justin.

"Justin!" I couldn't contain how excited I was to hear from him so soon.

"The big guys ended up finding out about some crew members who had been sleeping with guests and decided to drop the axe to try to stop lawsuits from guests." What did he mean by that?

"Did you get in trouble?" I didn't want to think I caused him any harm.

"I was fired, Lori." My chest felt empty, it was my fault. I was the one who pursued him.

"Justin."

"It's okay, I got back to my cabin and had a letter waiting for me from my boss." He explained. "I was off the ship about twenty minutes after you."

"Are you back in Australia?" I figured he would have gone home with his tail between his legs.

"That flight would have been longer than twenty-four hours." I guess it never occurred to me how long of a flight to Australia from Florida would be.

"Still in Fort Lauderdale?" There was a buzz at my door,

"Damn, someone's at the door. Hold on." I rushed to my intercom and without thinking just hit the enter button. I could have gotten into trouble with my association for not seeing who was at the door. "Are you still there, Justin?" I figured he was angry with me.

"Yes, and no, I left Florida as quickly as I could, I didn't want to stay there." He must have been on his way back to Australia on a layover.

I heard a knock on my door, "Okay, whoever was at the front door is now at *my* door."

"It's okay, I just reached where I needed to be anyway."

"At your gate? Have a safe rest of your flight, I miss you." The call ended as another knock echoed through my open-concept apartment, "I'll be right there." Part of me wished that this could be a romantic comedy where I would open the door and Justin would be there, but I was sure it was a package I had forgotten I ordered before the trip.

I reached the door nearly tripping over my suitcase and opened it, "Oh, my God."

It was Justin, standing at my door. "See, I'm where I need to be." He smiled with tears beginning to fall from his eyes.

"You came here?" I couldn't believe it, for the first time, I got a romantic comedy ending. I leaped into his arms and kissed him. As we kissed, I pulled him into my apartment, and he used his foot to shut the door.

I pulled away, "I'm so sorry."

Justin cocked his head, "For what?"

"You losing your job. It was my fault." I turned away from him.

He touched my shoulder which sent shivers up my back. "I ran that calculated risk." He kissed my neck. There was a sense of sadness in his voice. "I loved that job… but…"

I turned to face him, "But if it weren't for me, you wouldn't have lost a job you love."

Justin smiled, "But you see, there's this girl I love."

My heart fluttered at his words.

He pressed his forehead against mine, "I love you more than

that job." He kissed the tip of my nose and continued, "It took losing that job for me to realize how much I care for you."

My heart was beating so fast that I was worried Justin would hear it. "You have no idea how happy that makes me." I looked into his eyes, "Aren't you gonna miss it?"

Justin slightly nodded, "Sure, but I think I would miss you more." He pressed his lips against mine and we kissed. After our kiss, he asked, "Where's the bedroom?"

I took his hand and guided him to my bedroom.

An hour later, we cuddled under the covers of my bed. I played with his fingers interlocked with mine, "So, what do we do?" Now that the ship didn't separate us, we still had an ocean between our personal lives.

"I do need to head back to Australia for now, but I was planning on applying for a work visa and coming here to California to work."

"Where?" I had no idea how much thought he had put into this plan, but I wanted to know.

"Well, I loved the feeling of slinging drinks to people who were on vacation, and this area does have some good vacation spots." He brought our hands up to his face and gave me a very light kiss on my fingers.

"I do like Disney." I looked up and met his gaze.

"I like you." He answered as he kissed me again.

Neither one of us knew what was going to happen next, or how long he was going to be in Australia, before he could come back to me, "You know, I still haven't been to Australia." I smirked.

"Well, you haven't had time, but are you saying you want to come back with me? What about work?"

"My show is on hiatus right now, I have at least another month before I have to be back to work." I told him.

Justin smiled, "I usually like to date someone longer than a week before I have them meet my family." Was this his way of telling me that he didn't want me to come?

"Oh."

"I'll make an exception for you." He leaned in and kissed me again, this time deeply instead of a peck.

I felt his weight on me, and I couldn't imagine a better life than where it seemed to be heading this time. I had never cared for anyone as much as I had started caring for Justin.

After round two of our reunion, I slid out of my bed while he slept. I got on the computer and started looking for last-minute flights to Melbourne. "These aren't too bad," I whispered to myself as I scrolled through possible flights. I opened a new tab and started looking at photos of Melbourne. "It's a beautiful city." I noticed the Ferris Wheel off to the side, "Cool, it's like the London Eye."

I started to wonder what it would be like to move there after my show's inevitable end. It could be twenty years from now, or we could get a call tomorrow saying that it wasn't coming back.

I opened a third tab and started researching Australian cartoons, "Now, how could I take over Australian animation?" I learned more about Australia's animation past and more about its current existence.

"What are you looking at?" Justin was standing behind me in his boxers. I didn't even know he had gotten up.

"Oh, you startled me." I turned to him, "I guess, I'm just thinking what life would be like if I moved to Australia." I was hoping that didn't freak him out.

He kissed the top of my head, "I have no plans of moving back to Melbourne full time, I'm happy keeping it a place I go to celebrate Christmas."

"In summer, that's so weird." I smiled at him.

"Well, I've never had a white Christmas, so maybe we'll do Christmas with your family this year." He offered.

"Sure, since you've already met my family, you won't have that awkward meeting thing happening." I couldn't wait to not lie when I brought a boyfriend to a family event.

He looked out the window, "I like it here."

I smiled and looked at him, "And I love you..." My eyes

widened at my mistake. I didn't mean to blurt out an "I love you" this soon.

Justin turned back to me, "I love you too." He opened his arms welcoming me.

I collapsed into his arms. His warm embrace was the safest place in the world for me. "I know you do."

We kissed and hoped that this would be our happily ever after.

EPILOGUE
LORI

THREE YEARS LATER...

t was Christmas time. Justin and I flew in from California. My show had one final season before the network pulled the plug on it. Ryan took that opportunity to move to Minnesota to be with Derrek, Steph, and Benjamin.

They had decided to do long distance once we got word that the season after the cruise would be the end. Ryan ended up going back to school and becoming a chef.

Justin also went to school to get a visa to be in the States full-time. He decided to go into business so he could open his own bar. For now, he took on the idea of working at Disneyland as a bartender nights and weekends, and he loved it. It made seeing each other difficult, but we made it work.

Justin and I walked into Mom and Dad's house and saw the massive Christmas tree. Mom and I had spent time working on our relationship. Neither of us wanted it to end, so we ended up seeing a therapist together to help Mom and I understand each other.

"There they are!" Mom rushed over to me, and Dad took our luggage.

"Jack, the presents are in that bag." Justin pointed to the bag in Dad's left hand.

Mom hugged me and then Justin. "I'm so happy to finally have all my children back together again!" Mom walked into the kitchen. "Come on. We have appetizers out."

It didn't happen a lot, since I rarely came home from California. This Christmas, I had news. I had lied to my family again and had been for about a year. I turned to Justin, "Ready?"

Justin nodded, "Am I ready to stop keeping things from your family? Yes." He kissed me and we walked into the kitchen to join the rest of the family.

Steph sat at the kitchen table feeding her new baby under a blanket, "Hey!" She called out.

"Is that my new niece?" I walked up to her as she pulled little Gabbie from under the blanket, "It is." She looked to the hallway, "Honey, Lori's here!"

From the hallway leading to the bedrooms, in walked Ted. Ted was Steph's divorce lawyer. They ended up falling for each other, and when she was no longer his client, he asked her out for a drink which led to a wedding and a baby in the last two years. He was tall, muscular, and oh-so-dashingly handsome.

"Hey, Ted," I said with a smile.

"Hey Lori, Justin." Ted said as he reached his hand out to shake Justin's.

"Where's Ryan and Derrek?" I hadn't seen or heard them yet.

"Where do you think?" Steph asked with a knowing look.

I headed to the stairs leading to the basement. Mom and Dad had finished it off when we were kids and turned it into a kid's paradise. We had all the different gaming systems hooked up, there were dollhouses and stuffed animals. I walked down into the large downstairs living room and saw Derrek and Ryan, who had been married since Derrek's divorce with Steph was final. They ended up adopting a precious little girl that they named Julia.

All of Kasey's kids saw me and yelled in unison, "Auntie Lori!"

Benjamin raised his arms and shouted in baby something that sounded like "Aunt Lori" he was just copying his older cousins.

Ryan smiled at me then grabbed Julia's hands and raised them up, "Aunt Lori!"

"You should all come upstairs, I have something to tell you all."

Ryan looked at me, "Did you lie about your whole love life again?" He said as a joke.

"Kind of." I teased as I motioned my hand to make the group of children, and adult children, follow me.

Everyone sat in the living room confused, "What's going on and why am I not in on this?" Ryan asked.

"Well, as you all know, Justin went to school and got a second degree in business, well we had trouble keeping him in the States after that." I explained to them.

"The only way to do it was very quickly." Justin stopped.

"We got married about a year ago." I blurted out.

"You eloped?" My mother was so broken that she didn't get to help plan a big lavish wedding as she had for her other two kids, twice for Derrek.

"Yes, but, we want to, this summer, come back to Minnesota and throw a proper wedding," I explained.

"We felt guilty that none of you were there." Justin told them, "So, we're going to pretend like we aren't legally married and throw a massive party so all of us can celebrate together."

My dad stood with a proud look on his face. "We are so happy for you, and I would be happy to walk you down the aisle." He pulled me in for a hug and pulled Justin in as well.

"I promise to stop lying about my relationship status." I joked with my family.

"Good, because it's becoming a weird bad habit of yours." Kasey laughed.

"Well, the plan is that her relationship status is done changing," Justin said after the group hugs with my dad. He grabbed my hands and kissed me, "I love you."

"I love you too." I pulled him to the archway leading to the dining room and pointed up to the mistletoe.

"You know you don't need that to get me to kiss you." He leaned in and kissed me with our family watching. I was finally in love with the best partner I could have ever dreamed of. My dream man found me and my heart was full.

ABOUT THE AUTHOR

Britt Halaas is an author located in the Minneapolis area of Minnesota. She is a self-proclaimed pet parent millennial just trying to make it in the world. She has been a creative her whole life and dreams of doing it full-time one day. She is a body neutral fat person who wants to give fat women stories where they get to see themselves get the love stories they so rightfully deserve!

www.ingramcontent.com/pod-product-compliance
Lightning Source LLC
Chambersburg PA
CBHW061420160726

47995CB00003B/685